Priests in the United States

Books by Andrew M. Greeley:

And Young Men Shall See Visions
The Catholic Experience
The Changing Catholic College
The Church and the Suburbs
Come Blow Your Mind with Me
The Crucible of Change
The Education of Catholic Americans (with Peter H. Rossi)
The Friendship Game
A Future to Hope In
The Hesitant Pilgrim: American Catholicism After the Council
The Jesus Myth
Letters to Nancy
Life for a Wanderer
New Horizons for the Priesthood
Priests in the United States
A Profile of Catholic Higher Education
Religion and Career
Religion in the Year 2000
Strangers in the House
Uncertain Trumpet
What a Modern Catholic Believes About God
What We Believe (with Martin Marty and Stuart Rosenberg)
Why Can't They Be Like Us? Ethnic Conflict in America

Priests in the United States

REFLECTIONS ON A SURVEY

Andrew M. Greeley

Doubleday & Company, Inc.

Garden City, New York

1972

Library of Congress Catalog Card Number 75–175378
Copyright © 1972 by Andrew M. Greeley
All Rights Reserved
Printed in the United States of America
First Edition

CONTENTS

Priests in the United States

INTRODUCTION

This book is intended to present a series of reflections on the recent study of the American Catholic priesthood by the National Opinion Research Center. It is neither a research report nor a technical monograph; a research report has already been submitted to the client,[1] and a technical monograph for the social science profession is in preparation. However, if there is one thing I have learned in my years as a sociologist, it is that the researcher who gets involved in controversial projects has not discharged his obligation when he has submitted a report to his client and a monograph to his colleagues. His findings will be read and interpreted by the general public (even if the client does his best to keep the report away from the public), and frequently those findings will be distorted beyond all possible recognition. The scholar must, I think, present his own interpretations about what his research means, not as the only possible interpretation, not even as the definitive interpretation, but as an interpretation which must be dealt with. If I had it to do over again, I would not have failed to provide an interpretation for the NORC parochial school study.[2] I do not believe the conscientious researcher can merely wash his hands of a project when he submits the report. He cannot, of course, have any direct influence on the policy decisions which are based on the report, but by reflecting on it and interpreting the meaning of his findings he can set up a context within which others can

[1] This report, *American Priests*, was prepared for the National Conference of Catholic Bishops.
[2] Andrew M. Greeley and Peter H. Rossi, *Education of Catholic Americans* (Garden City, N.Y., Doubleday & Company, Inc., 1968).

judge whether given policy decisions or recommendations do in fact flow inevitably from the research findings.

There is something of self-defense in such behavior on the part of the researcher: He wishes to protect his research from being misused and his own professional reputation from being co-opted—whether by the right or the left (in whatever shape these two groups may manifest themselves in a given controversy). There is no getting away from the truth that if research findings are torn out of context to support a policy which the data in fact do not support, the researcher and the research are indeed being misused.

The research on the impact of Catholic education was badly misused both by the supporters and the opponents of Catholic schools (more by the latter, since few supporters bothered to read the report). I presume that the research on the Catholic priesthood will also be misused; but this time, I am going to make it more difficult for those who preface their own biased decisions with "The NORC report says . . ."

The research report *American Priests* contains no recommendations. It is a matter of ordinary policy at NORC not to make recommendations in any research report unless constrained by a client to do so. There was no such constraint in the study of the priesthood. My own feeling is that it was just as well, because the experience of most researchers shows that the likelihood of the research report being accepted is in inverse relationship to the number of recommendations made. In the present volume I will engage in a good deal more speculation than my colleagues and I on the NORC team did in *American Priests*. I shall not hesitate to make recommendations. I shall make careful distinctions between the research findings, my own speculations on them, and recommendations which I think might be appropriately drawn from both findings and speculations. While I think that both the speculations and recommendations of this book are reasonable reflections and conclusions from the research material, I wish to emphasize that they do not flow from the research findings with any inevitable logic; they are my own, no one else's, and I have no doubt that another man of competence and good will could read the data differently. I also wish to emphasize that I am speaking for myself, not for my colleagues of the National Opinion Research Center, some of whom might also write different sets of reflections on the priesthood study.

I am not writing these reflections to support the ideological position either of those who advocate major changes in the American priesthood or those who oppose such changes. On the contrary, my sentiments about both sides of the controversy tend to be that of the young man in *Romeo and Juliet* who had the misfortune of getting caught between the Montagues and the Capulets in a street fight.

I refuse to be forced into taking a position that will ally me either with some of the members of the board of directors of the National Federation of Priests' Councils or some of the delegates to the National Conference of Catholic Bishops for the Synod in Rome. As a matter of fact, I don't see much to choose between the two groups, for neither seem to have much awareness of the complexities of the human condition or the human person. I have long since discovered that the important political and social distinctions are not between men who are liberals and conservatives but between men who think the world is simple and those who know it is not. I side with the latter.

If I do not have an ideological position, I do have a perspective from which my reflections in the present book will be taken. It is important, I think, to make clear both my religious and sociological perspectives.

1. Religious Perspective

a. I believe that the core of Christianity is a message, a message of God's loving mercy which manifested itself by His decisive intervention in human history in the person and the words of Jesus of Nazareth.

b. I believe that the Church is a community of those who have accepted that message and dedicated themselves to spreading it.

c. I believe that the priest is *ex officio* the leader of that religious community, and that like all other religious leaders human societies have known, his fundamental leadership responsibility is preaching and interpreting the message.

d. Therefore, I take it that the priest is a man of conviction, a man of faith.

e. I am further convinced that the religious convictions which a priest stands for have certain inevitable social consequences. A priest cannot separate himself from the human condition; he must be concerned with problems of suffering and misery wherever he finds them. The priest as therapist or the priest as social reformer is, in my view of things, a very proper figure so long as it is not forgotten that his therapy and reform are a consequence of his religious faith and not a substitute for it.

f. If social involvement is not a substitute for faith, so faith and enthusiasm are no substitutes for competence. If I had to choose between a dedicated man without competence and a competent man without conviction, I would choose the latter. The competent man may become apathetic, but the incompetent man may become fanatical, and the world has seen too many fanatics.

2. Sociological Perspectives

a. I am convinced that there are no simple problems or simple solutions in the modern world, and that however much admirable energy may be generated by simplistic moralizing, such energy is probably a liability to the cause of social reform.

b. I am also persuaded that in most sets of circumstances the pace of social change will be relatively slow. Given the fact that our personalities and values are shaped largely in childhood and adolescent experiences, value changes in society and consequent structural reforms frequently must wait for new generations to appear rather than for older generations to be converted.

c. I have a strong distaste for clichémongering. I wince when every new movement representing a tiny fraction of some sub population group is called a "revolution." Similarities between the great cataclysms of Paris in 1789, Dublin in 1916, and Leningrad in 1917, and anything presently happening in the American republic or the American Catholic Church are pretty hard to find.

d. I have profound respect for the importance of scholarship, particularly in a time of sudden and unexpected change. A scholar's ability to see the various sides of the question, to explore the historical roots of the problem, and to ponder the various implications of possible future developments is desperately needed in a time when the simple-minded clichémonger tends to dominate the scene. (It is particularly tragic to see scholars abandon their scholarly pose to become clichémongers themselves in a desperate and usually fruitless quest for "relevance.")

e. I have a deep respect for tradition. Whether we all like it or not, we are products of our own past. The secret of sound and healthy growth is not the denial of the past but understanding what is positive and constructive in the past and building upon it. There were many things wrong with immigrant Catholicism in the United States, but there were also some things that were right with it, and the possibilities for growth in the American Catholic Church in years to come will depend largely on the ability of leadership and scholarship to facilitate a transition from the structures of immigrant Catholicism to those of postimmigrant, post-Conciliar form of Catholicism. I must confess that at the present time I am not too optimistic about this happening.

f. Finally, I am suspicious about the tendency for elites (particularly journalistic elites) to read into a large population group what they and their friends believe the large population groups *ought* to think. The tendency of some Catholic lay journalists to assume the mantle of "spokesmen" for the Catholic laity would be amusing if it were in jest, but as serious social analysis it is rather sad.

It is not my intention to argue about these assumptions, for they are mine and I propose to operate within the context they create. If the reader does not like the assumptions, that is both his privilege and his problem, but if he reads on in the book, he would be much better advised to criticize me for departing from the context of my own assumptions rather than for having them in the first place.

I will not attempt to justify social research or defend the competence and intelligence of NORC as a research organization. Nor will I explain the theory and technology of the priesthood study; I will assume that anyone who has bothered to purchase this book is willing to concede that social research does get at reality, however crudely and incompletely, and that he will also concede that NORC, the nation's oldest social research organization, is both competent and honest. If he is incurably interested in the theory and methodology of the study, he will read about it in the research report itself.

I will also try to keep at a minimum tables, percentages, and that marvelous new plaything of the sociologists, the path analysis diagram. I don't think that either tables or path diagrams are all that arcane, but I am convinced that social scientists ought to be able to talk about their research without depending on the jargon or the apparatus of their professions, especially since many readers are frightened away when they see a vast array of statistical tables.

In all but one of the subsequent chapters I will present three separate sections:

1) *Findings:* The principal factual data on the given subject will be summarized in a series of propositions. These summary propositions have the full weight of NORC's research effort behind them and can be substantiated by the tables and ap-

pendices of our report to the National Conference of Catholic Bishops.[3]

2) *Speculations:* In this section of each chapter I will offer my own ideas about the causes, implications, and likely future effects of our findings. I will speak no longer for NORC or with the certainty of "hard" statistical data. I will speak of course as a sociologist who worked two years on the survey and who has spent a good many years studying the American Church. I'm sure the other sociologists—including I daresay my colleagues on the survey staff—would draw different conclusions. The reader is warned therefore that he is dealing with one man's ideas and opinions in the "speculations" sections of each chapter.

3) *Recommendations:* In this section I will become even less "scientific" and more "personal" and advocate certain policy changes which seemed to me to be appropriate in light of the findings presented in the first section and the analysis offered in the second section. I am not a policy maker—and not likely ever to be one—in the American Church; nor do the present group of policy makers seem likely ever to seek my advice. I offer my unsolicited and unwanted advice if only to provide the reader with a model against which he can decide what recommendations *he* thinks would be most appropriate—not that the policy makers give a hoot what the average reader thinks either.

The principal weakness of the present research on the Catholic priesthood is that nobody has bothered to speak to the clients. In the original proposal made to the National Conference of Cath-

---

[3] It must be noted here that all the findings which I mention are a matter of public record, released in the summary distributed to the press by the National Conference of Catholic Bishops. At the present writing the NCCB has not released the complete text of the report. I will not violate my professional commitments by repeating any factual material not contained in the official summary. However, no major or important finding was omitted from the summary. I do not know why the NCCB has delayed the release of the report, but it cannot have been to hide the unpleasant findings. For all the findings which might have been embarrassing to the NCCB are already on the record.

olic Bishops it was urged that a study of the laity's attitudes toward the priesthood be undertaken at the same time as the study of the priests themselves. Unfortunately, it was not deemed financially possible to attempt the two studies simultaneously, and one can scarcely be optimistic at the present about the likelihood of a study of the Catholic laity now.

If there is any fundamental theme to hold together the reflections of this book, it is that the Catholic priesthood in the United States has many strong, positive assets but also some critical problems which, if they are not resolved, make the long-run prospects for the priesthood look rather bleak.

I

BACKGROUND

1. Catholic priests come from a somewhat higher social class background than typical American Catholics. Their fathers had somewhat better jobs, and both fathers and mothers had somewhat better education than did the parents of typical American Catholic males. However, these differences hardly mean that priests come from a completely different social class than their parishioners. Thirty-one per cent of the priests had fathers who had at least graduated from high school, as did 23 per cent of the American Catholic males.

2. Much of this social class difference is in reality an ethnic difference. The Irish are 17 per cent of the Catholic population, 35 per cent of the Catholic priesthood, and 50 per cent of the Catholic hierarchy. The Italians are the principal underrepresented group in the clergy. They are 19 per cent of the Catholic population (the largest of all American ethnic groups) and only 5 per cent of the clergy and 3 per cent of the hierarchy.

3. There seems to be no relationship between age and the ethnic distribution of the American clergy. Despite the widespread impression that some seminaries have far more Italian and Polish students than Irish students, the overrepresentation of the Irish and the underrepresentation of the Italians is as true among the clergy between twenty-six and thirty-five as it is in

all other age groups. If there is a shift of the Irish away from the seminary and an Italian and Polish shift toward it, it has not yet made itself felt in the ethnic distribution of even the youngest age cohort of priests.

4. Most priests come from very devout Catholic families. However, there is a relationship between family tension in one's past and resignation from the priesthood. As we shall see later in our discussion of resignation, this correlation is not high (.2),[1] but it does persist. Priests from relatively tense family backgrounds are more likely to leave the priesthood because they are less likely to get satisfaction from prayer, more likely to have "modern religious values," and more likely to experience loneliness.

5. Three fifths of the American clergy graduated from high school before entering the seminary.

6. Two thirds of the clergy report that their seminary prepared them at least moderately well for the ministry, though majorities said their seminary instructions were too theoretical and irrelevant to pastoral needs and agreed that the seminary was too sheltered from the problems of the world and that few attempts were made to teach seminarians how to deal with people. Only about one third of the priests of the country approved of high school seminaries, although three fifths of the bishops were in favor of such seminaries.

7. One quarter of the American priests dated at least two or three times a month before entering the seminary, and 60 per cent of them had some kind of dating experience before becoming seminarians.

8. The most important influences in the decision to become

[1] A correlation coefficient is the measure of relationship between two variables. It indicates the relationship between the position of respondents on one variable and their position on another variable. The square of the correlation coefficient is the indication of the amount of variance explained in the relationship. Thus a correlation of .7 between age and height for teen-agers would mean that 49 per cent of the variance of teen-agers on a continuum measuring their height can be explained by their position on a continuum measuring age.

a priest were another priest (mentioned by a little more than two fifths of our respondents) and the priest's mother (mentioned by one third of the respondents).

9. While there is a strong relationship between dating and the time of entering the seminary (the earlier men entered the seminary, the less dating they report), there is no relationship between time of entry and any other important variables in our study. Only one relationship between dating and other variables was found: a .2 relationship between dating and one's score on an inner-directed personality scale (which we will discuss in the following chapter). In other words, there is no connection between the age at which one entered the seminary and emotional maturity, satisfaction with the priesthood, attitudes toward authority, morale, loneliness, desire to marry, or propensity to leave the priesthood. Whether one dated or not explains only 4 per cent of the variants on the measure of emotional maturity.

SPECULATIONS

1. The End of the Immigrant Church

The most fundamental demographic fact about American Catholicism is that it is still but one generation away from the immigrant experience. In 1963, at the time of the parochial school study, 10 per cent of the American adult Catholic population had been born abroad and another 40 per cent were the children of immigrants. (Interestingly enough, about 10 per cent of the priests were also born abroad, a figure which does *not* correlate with age.) The immigrant experience is still too close to us for us to be able to get a proper perspective on it, hence we ignore it. I am unaware of any serious discussion in the last decade of the impact of the immigration experience on the structure and ethos of American Catholicism. It has been argued, of course, that we must leave behind immigrant Catholicism, but that assumes one can leave behind an immigrant experience which historically speaking occurred almost the day before yesterday. It is also interesting to note that virtually no Catholic intellectual or journalist has been involved in the revival of interest in ethnicity currently so fashionable among academic, government, and foundation elites. For most American Catholics, the ethnic immigrant neighborhood is still too much a part of their own past for them to want to rediscover it or to remember it. It may take another generation before American Catholics are able to understand what the overwhelming fact of immigration meant in the first half—or even the first three quarters—of the twentieth century.

However, there are two dimensions of the immigration experience that must be kept in mind in any consideration of the American Catholic Church: (1) The immigrant wants to "make it" in the new society. He wants to prove that he is as good an American as anyone else. (2) At the same time, he does not wish to lose completely either continuity with his past or membership in the supportive community of his fellow immigrants. Thus, the immigrant is torn in two directions: toward assimilation on the one hand and toward some kind of cultural segregation on the other. The American solution, at least in theory, has been to extol the merits of cultural pluralism, of acculturation which does not demand assimilation. In practice, however, we have generally insisted on the glories of the "melting pot," and have been prepared to concede that it is all right for those who have come in after us (whoever "we" happen to be) to be different so long as they are not very different; which is to say that it is all right to be different so long as we can be confident that the differences are rapidly disappearing. The recent insistence by black people on their own form of cultural pluralism (which is, in effect, what black pride really is)[2] has once again brought the question of cul-

2 L. Paul Metzger, "American Sociology and Black Assimilation: *Conflicting Perspectives*," *American Journal of Sociology*, Vol. 76, No. 4 (January 1971), pp. 628–44.

tural pluralism in American society into sharp focus. Characteristically, the reaction of mainstream America is to see black cultural pluralism as a form of neosegregationist separatism, which it is not, as any cursory examination of surveys of black attitudes indicates.

The importance of the dilemma of the melting pot versus cultural pluralism for American priests ought to be obvious, but since it appears from most discussions of the priesthood that it is not obvious, the point must be made explicit: Virtually all priests over forty grew up, were educated, prepared for the ministry, and served in parishes in which the social ambience was created by the strain between assimilation and pluralism. Priests over thirty were for the most part trained in seminaries which were established to service an immigrant Church. Most priests are still led by religious leaders who must work in formal structures that were strongly influenced by the immigrant phenomenon. Finally, the overwhelming majority of parishioners of American priests are not nearly as liberated from the conflicts and tensions of the immigrant experience as the Catholic elites would like to believe. It is fashionable to assume that there is no discrimination against Poles and Italians in American society, but most Poles and Italians would know better. It is fashionable to assert that the immigrant era has come to an end, but any priest who takes a serious look around his own diocese, particularly if it is a large urban diocese in the northeast or north-central part of the country, is only too well aware that the immigrant era is still with us—dying out, of course, but slowly; and as in every case of social change, the structures of immigrant Catholicism are dying less rapidly than the immigrant experience itself.

The conservatism, the fear, the suspicion, the clannish loyalty, the narrowness, which are typical of any immigrant experience, shaped American Catholicism, perhaps decisively, until the great turning point of 1960 when John F. Kennedy was elected President. But the immigrant mentality did not go away in

1960, and neither did the immigrants and their children. Even without the Vatican Council the Church would have found itself caught in the extremely difficult strain of having one foot in the immigrant neighborhood and another foot in the upper middle-class suburb (while straddling the "in between" community of the blue-collar suburb). The change from the post-Tridentine to the post-Vatican Church has been more abrupt but no more complete than the change from the "old neighborhood" to the suburb. The cautious, stable, unquestioning immigrant parish harmonized nicely with the cautious, stable, conservative post-Tridentine Church. Furthermore, it was extremely difficult for an immigrant community to produce its own intelligentsia. (The Jews did it, of course, but to some extent they brought their intelligentsia with them—something that the Irish were unable to do, since theirs had a way of getting itself destroyed.) Hence, American Catholicism, for all its colleges and universities, was not plugged in to the intellectual communications networks of Western Europe and, so, completely unprepared for the dramatic theological changes taking place before the Vatican Council ratified and re-enforced them. The Vatican Council burst upon the American Church like a bombshell for which no one was prepared.

The overwhelming majority of American Catholics, lay and clerical alike, were raised in an immigrant Counter Reformation Church, and even if they wanted to (and there is no evidence that many of them do), they cannot put aside the attitudes, styles, and values they learned in their formative years. American priests at the present and in the years to come are necessarily going to have to live with a transitional situation, a transition for themselves (unless they are very young) and for their parishioners. It would be nice if the transition with all its confusion and ambiguity could be ended now, but to merely announce that it is over will not end it. The American clergy will have to learn to live with ambiguity and uncertainty for a good long time to come.

But the trouble is that they were not trained to cope with ambiguity and uncertainty. The family structure, primary and secondary educations, seminary preparation, and values and models of parochial life assumed immutability and stability which, however much some priests complained about it, provided a reassuring psychological and social context. I am inclined to think that much of the talk about a clerical culture is exaggerated. What we had in fact was an immigrant culture in which the role of the clergy was defined as much by the fact that the priests were the leaders of the immigrant community as it was by the fact that they had a sacred role to play. If the culture of the clergy was now inward-looking and parochial, it was merely the reflection of a larger culture which, given its recent arrival on American shores (or should one say its recent birth on American shores?) could not be anything other than what it was.

The change, one assumes, from immigrant to postimmigrant Catholicism and from Byzantine to Vatican Catholicism would have occurred in any event. What the Vatican Council did was to accelerate the process dramatically. Instead of slow and gradual (perhaps too slow and too gradual) transition, the change of the American Church was dramatic and abrupt; and in the absence of scholarly preparation for it and a leadership adroit enough to see its implications, the change was traumatic. The only theory that American Catholicism had was to protect the faith of the immigrants and their children while they acculturated to a new world, and the only leadership it had was a leadership trained in protecting the Church from external enemies. It was impossible to expect that there would have been much scholarship to talk not so much about where the Church was as about where it came from and whither it was going, and a leadership concerned with directing and focusing enormous energies instead of protection and defense. It was impossible to expect that there would have been any such scholarship available. Given the decline in the quality of the leadership of the

American Church since the turn of the century crisis in relationships with Rome, and the careful surveillance of the apostolic delegate after that crisis, it would have been naïve to
expect appropriate leadership either. The crisis in the American
Church, and especially the crisis in the priesthood, has about it
the inevitability of a Greek tragedy.

If one is going to understand the present problems of the
American priesthood, one must realize that it has experienced
in the last decade an extraordinarily severe trauma in which
the values, the behavior patterns, the leadership styles, and the
goals of the past were jettisoned almost overnight. In the absence
of both the theory and the leadership to facilitate the acquisition
of new styles, chaos is not too strong a word for the result.
What is surprising is not that there have been confusion and
disarray in the clergy but that the strength and morale of the
clergy have persisted at the relatively high levels described in
subsequent chapters.

But the transition from immigrant to postimmigrant Catholicism involves other problems besides the question of clerical
identity and the conflict of leadership styles between older and
younger generations. Even more important is the fact that the
transition trauma has hit the clergy far more sharply than the
laity. Religion is the business of the clergy. They are the ones
expected to be most informed about it. They are the ones who
are plugged into those communications networks that keep them
posted on the latest changes and the most recent fashions. A dramatic change in the posture of the Church will be communicated
to and affect the clergy far more quickly than the laity. Hence
the American priests, and particularly younger priests, are likely
to be far more involved in the post-Vatican "thing" than are
the laity. The typical layman can only allot a certain portion
of his time and interest to keeping pace with religious change.
Even the young lay person, in most circumstances, is not at-
tuned to the most recent religious categories and styles. With
change going on much faster in the clergy than the laity,
there is bound to be tension between clergy and laity, a tension

which never existed before in the American Church. Fundamentally the problem is that many of the clergy are busy attempting to redefine their roles to fit the new theories (or sometimes fads) which they are hearing. The laity, for their part, may not have heard the theories, or if they have heard them, may not have understood them. They are not sure they like the role redefination, especially if they have been given no opportunity to participate in the redefinition. There is an interesting paradox here, for in the pre-1960 Church the position of the priest was such that he could do pretty much what he wanted without bothering to consult the laity (build a new church, a new school, change the mass schedule, etc.). Now, in the post-1960 Church, the clergyman is expected to consult the laity. But, in fact, many priests, it seems, are trying to redefine their own roles in the pre-1960 style, and then to present the new role to the lay people as an accomplished fact. The laity, understandably enough, are puzzled.

The above speculation has not, of course, been documented by any research on the attitudes of the American laity. It really must stand as hypotheses for further research, hypotheses, however, which social theory would lead us to believe ought to enjoy a good deal of plausibility.

In summary, the American priesthood has two problems as it moves into the present phase of acculturation of American immigrant groups. (1) It must accomplish a transition in defining its own role, a transition which most priests did not expect and were unprepared to make. (2) At the same time it must cope with the fact that the transition among its lay clientele is likely to proceed at a much slower rate than its own. There are, then, two powerful sets of ambiguities which must be dealt with by men most of whom were trained for a very unambiguous set of responsibilities.

2. The Irish Church

With half the hierarchy and almost two fifths of the clergy Irish, there can be no doubt that the impress of Irish Catholicism on the American Church is strong. In many ways, such an impact is not unfortunate. A closeness between priests and people, intense loyalty to the organization, an understanding of Anglo-Saxon ways, and a political shrewdness which enabled one to exploit to the fullest the weakness of the host society —all of these stood the American Church in good stead in the early phases of the immigrant experience. The poetic, mystical, intellectual, and literary strains of Irish culture seem somehow to have been lost in the immigrant transition, at least after Rome destroyed the progressive wing of the American hierarchy at the end of the nineteenth century. However, in the great bishop of Charleston John England, one has at least a historical symbol of what might have developed in the way of a liberal, intellectual Irish Catholicism if the historical fates (and the decisions of the Roman Curia) had been different.

On balance, there is no reason to think that Irish Catholicism is any more narrow, parochial, or authoritarian than another ethnic religious tradition which, if the circumstances had been different, might have shaped the development of the American Church. (And here historians will note that I disagree strongly with the suggestion of the late Father Thomas McAvoy, the noted historian, that native American Catholicism might have been more sophisticated and more liberal than the Irish Catholicism which replaced it. Rome would have stomped down the native American Catholicism of John Ireland just as readily as it crushed the Irish liberals.)

The real problem of the Irish shape of American Catholicism is one that is rarely mentioned in serious Catholic journals: the relationship of the Irish to the ethnic immigrants that came after them. One would have thought that having escaped from the horrendous political oppression they knew in Ireland, the Irish would have been sympathetic with the other oppressed groups which followed them to the New World. In fact, however, we know enough psychological theory to realize that a basically insecure group does not have the emotional resources it needs to be tolerant of another group still less secure and accepted. For all too many of the leaders of the American Church, past and present, to be an American Catholic meant to be an Irish Catholic. Acculturation into American society was taken to mean the same thing as acculturation to Irish Catholicism. Needless to say, other immigrant groups did not readily accept such standards, and they were not especially pleased with the "separate but equal" status the Irish clergy conceded them in the form of the national parish. Nevertheless, the Irish ploy may have been successful. A number of Italian scholars have observed—not altogether enthusiastically—that third-generation Italians become more and more "Irish" in their religious style. However, the new emphasis on ethnic consciousness may change all of this. One detects among some Polish and Italian clergy a new openness and militancy in their hostility toward Irish Catholic domination. Furthermore, it may well be that the Irish because of their better education will more quickly acquire the styles of the post-Vatican Church (a better education, be it noted, is almost entirely the result of the fact that the Irish were here first). In which case, the situation could develop where the conflict between the clergy and the laity would be based not only on the more rapid transition among the former but on a combination of a rapid transition to new ecclesiastical styles and ethnic hostility. A middle-aged Polish priest might say, "Not only is this young priest trying to make me abandon a cherished religious tradition, he is also Irish and trying to make me stop being Polish." Conventional wisdom says that this sort of conflict should have vanished thirty years ago. Maybe it has, but no serious observer of contemporary American Catholicism can afford to be confident on the subject.

3. The Seminary as Scapegoat

I yield to no one in my retrospective resentment for what was done to me during my seminary years. It was an extraordinarily unpleasant experience, one which was effectively if not deliberately designed to induce a state of permanent dependence on father figures. Nonetheless, I am impressed by the fact that we find no relationship between the number of years spent in the seminary and any important variable in the present attitudes and behavior of priests. I am equally impressed by the fact, to be reported in a subsequent chapter, that the products of Catholic seminaries score no lower on measures of self-actualization than do other Americans of the same age. It could be, of course, that the length of time one spends in the seminary really doesn't matter, that one year has as much impact as seven. Nevertheless, the absence of a relationship between time spent in the seminary and present attitudes and behavior, combined with the fact that priests tend to be as self-actualizing (or as nonself-actualizing), leads me to suspect that however important the seminary is as a scapegoat for present problems in the priesthood, it is not in fact a major cause of those problems.

On the contrary, I am inclined to think that the seminary was an effect rather than cause, that it reflected the values, structures, and styles of immigrant Catholicism rather than creating them. What American priests are, in other words, is much more likely to be the result of their experiences in the family than their experiences in the seminary, and of the culture of immigrant Catholicism rather than the clerical culture of the seminary. As one psychotherapist who had dealt at great length with priests told me, "I only become really confident about possibilities of growth when a priest begins to realize that his problems antedate his entering the seminary."

I am not suggesting, of course, that there was no need for seminary reform; clearly, there was, but the question is largely academic now, for the old seminary system has collapsed, to be replaced by the present chaos. I am asserting that the success of the old seminary in molding us to its ways was rooted in substantial part on the fact that it was but the logical continuation of the family structure and the culture in which we were raised. The seminary came apart at the seams only when it began to receive young men whose childhood experiences were drastically different from that of the seminarians who preceded them. I shed no tear for the seminary of the past, but I think it is shallow and superficial analysis that persists in seeing the seminary as the major villain, great father-surrogate that it was, the seminary was fated to be the object of a love/hate syndrome for most of its alumni.

4. The Seminary as Identity Crisis.

The seminary system was one of the first of the structures of immigrant Tridentine Catholicism to collapse. Such a phenomenon was inevitable, both because the seminary came into early contact with the new upper middle-class American Catholic, and because the seminary faculty, dealing as it did with ideas (more or less), was more likely to hear the ideas of the post-Vatican Church than other clergy were. There is no better example of what happens to an institution in change when it lacks both leadership and scholarship than the disasters which have afflicted the American seminary system. It is no exaggeration to say that American seminaries have not had the foggiest idea of where they were going, what they were for, or what they ought to be doing for the last ten years. The result has been a frenzy of activity with ever increasing confusion, disorganization, and discouragement. Studies have been made (a "study" usually means that some outside expert is called upon to make the decisions that in previous eras were attributed to the Holy Spirit), plans were adopted, grandiose new designs were produced, buildings were constructed then abandoned, and, above all, "movement" became necessary.

Seminaries were combined, only to have the combinations part; seminaries were moved to secular college campuses or, more recently, to divinity schools on the dubious premise that the university campus and/or the divinity school were places where "reality" could be found. Each new master plan, each new dramatic move was hailed as the wave of the future, the final development, the new method of training the clergy. I once remonstrated with a seminary rector about a change he proposed to make that seemed to me ill-advised. I thought he had neither the theoretical perspective nor the research data to justify the change. His response was "We've got to do something. Nobody here can tolerate all the confusion." Of course the "something" they did only made the confusion worse, but the passion for closure, for solution, or, in other words, for a return to the stability of the past is very strong. One can scarcely criticize the seminary system for wishing to experiment, but foolish experimentation based on nothing more than instinct or passing fashion, entered into quickly and abandoned more quickly, can scarcely be credited as an effective solution to anything. Seminary leadership frequently turns to the students for guidance, since it is assumed that the students, being young, will know what ought to be done. Indeed, the students will not hesitate to offer their rather dogmatic convictions on the subject of seminary training. The only trouble is that these convictions change even more rapidly than those of their teachers and administrators.

The latest fashion is the so-called clinical-pastoral training. This means that the seminarian hies himself to a hospital, prison, or mental institution where he is supposed to get practical experience by dealing with the kinds of people and the sorts of situations which he will almost never encounter when working in a parish. Whether the "clinical-pastoral" fashion will last any longer than the others is certainly problematic.

It is not my intention to deny that there is merit in the idea of clinical-pastoral training. The seminary is in some ways a professional school, and it is appropriate that professionals get some kind of supervised training in the exercise of the skills of their profession. Many of the people involved in the clinical-pastoral approach are talented men. My criticism is not so much clinical-pastoral training itself as it is of the mindless

enthusiasm by which it has been embraced. Unless a clear
theoretical notion is derived as to what a priest ought to be
doing, and unless a clear vision is developed of what kind of
training is appropriate for what he ought to be doing, piece-
meal, ad hoc, faddist innovations are doomed to failure before
they start, precisely because there will be insufficient motivation
to stick at these innovations when they encounter those problems
contingent on all human effort demanding coordination and
organization.

Futhermore, unless comprehensive research is done on the
reasons for the decline in vocations, any seminary planning for
the future is an absurdity. The resolute refusal of the leadership
of the Church in general and the seminaries in particular to
replace private opinion on the vocation crisis with serious research is a measure of just how confused the American Church
really is.

And so the fads and fashions continue as seminarians and
seminary faculty desperately seek a place where they can find
relevance, "where the action is," where people will "tell it like
it is" (which generally means "tell it like they have decided it is
without bothering to investigate"). Recently, St. Mary of the
Lake Seminary, my own alma mater (about which I have
appropriately ambivalent feelings), contemplated a move from
suburban Mundelein to Hyde Park in Chicago in order that it
might cuddle up with the great maternal figure of the University
of Chicago. The faculty and administration of that seminary
are among the most sensitive and most sophisticated in the
country. Without being asked, I ventured to inquire the reasons
for the move. Apparently it was felt that Hyde Park was a
center of action, both ecumenical and social, and by moving
in to a place both inner city and university, the faculty and
students of the seminary would come into contact with a "real,
intellectual community." My opinion, not sought but given
anyway, was that Hyde Park was a drab, dirty, dull, dangerous,
dismal place, and no one in his right mind would live there
unless he had to. To trade a couple of thousand acres of

splendid green land in northern Illinois for an apartment building
or a converted hotel in Hyde Park was foolishness—especially
when the latest student elite was moving out of the city back
into the countryside. Hyde Park was not an intellectual community; it was simply a neighborhood where intellectuals happened to live—when they weren't on sabbaticals. Opportunity
for faculty and students to rub shoulders with the divinity
school greats was not likely to be any more extensive than
the opportunities afforded divinity school students or even colleagues. I insisted that we intellectuals have a way of doing our
own things as far away as possible from both our colleagues
and students.

My friends at Mundelein listened politely, and it dawned on
me that the power of the Hyde Park mythology was so great
that they simply did not believe me. At such times, one is
tempted to rant and rave the truth of one's assertions. I re-
strained myself.

For reasons which had nothing to do with my intervention,
Mundelein didn't move to Hyde Park. Instead it did the very
sensible and intelligent thing of setting up a small outpost in
that bastion of high culture to see what developed. Would
that such intelligent experiments had preceded all the other
dramatic shifts that have taken place in other seminaries in the
past decade.

I must confess that I am especially skeptical of the proximity-
to-divinity-school syndrome. As high as my admiration is for the
faculty of our divinity school at the University of Chicago,
I think it has caused a great deal of problems for our Protestant
brothers, problems which they haven't really admitted to themselves as yet. Given half an opportunity, the divinity school
syndrome will produce vast problems for us, too.[3] There is no

[3] As Jaroslav Pelikan once remarked to me, "You people are trying
to make the same mistakes in twenty-five years that it took us four
hundred and fifty years to make." Pelikan was wrong. We should be able
to compress the thing into ten or fifteen years.

place on a university campus where the stereotypical snobbishness of the liberal academic is more powerful than in the divinity school. Feeling themselves to be on the margins of the university community, the divinity school faculty and students are strongly motivated to overadjust to what they think is the appropriate style of belief and behavior for an authentic academic. Despite (and maybe because of) their dealing with the soft, not to say mushy, disciplines of theology, the divinity school faculty member and his students want to say to the other denizens of the university, "See, we can be as much liberal academic as you are." This means that the divinity school is likely to be the site of the most recent fashion but one. With all their desperate attempts to keep up with what the real intellectuals are saying, they are never quite able to catch the avant-garde. What is likely to emerge from the divinity school—for all the required clinical-pastoral training—is a caricature of the liberal intellectual graduate student, in most instances complete with contempt for the vast range of American society save that occupied by the currently fashionable messianic group (in the 1960s, the blacks, in the 1930s, the working man). The divinity school graduate learns, more by osmosis than direct instruction, that the vast majority of middle Americans, that is to say, his future parishioners, are white racist polluter hawks, with whom it will be impossible for him to work and still keep any of his prophetic integrity. It is therefore necessary for him to denounce these uncouth semiliterate savages and demand of them that they obtain salvation by acknowledging their guilt for war, pollution, and racism. It is further necessary that he maintain his own personal integrity by keeping alert to the latest liberal intellectual fashions as they come down the pike and join the ranks before they march too far ahead. (Fortunately, by reading *The Christian Century*, he can pull this off with relative ease.) It is unfortunate that one is rarely effective in working with people of whom one is contemptuous and denunciation almost never changes anyone's mind.

Having been cheated of the advantages of university divinity school training, most Catholic clergy have been able to maintain a much better relationship with their laity than have many of the ministers of the elite Protestant denominations. However, as the credentials of a liberal academic become ever more important for assignment to a Catholic parish, one can reasonably anticipate that the alienation between clergy and laity, that scholars like Jeffrey Hadden report exist within the Protestant clergy, will also increase in the Catholic clergy. Alas, when that happens, the Catholic clergy are likely to be so convinced of their own moral righteousness that they will never bother to ask themselves whether they are listening to what their people say and mark them down as bigots simply because they are inarticulate or cannot mouth the latest liberal academic jargon.

I do not think future priests should be excused from developing their powers of thought and expression—which I take to be the goal of university training. I am arguing, on the contrary, that it is of the utmost importance that their powers of thought and expression be developed to the extent that they are able to break through the clichés and the fashions of whatever environment they find themselves in, including those of academe.

I am not hopeful about the present situation of American seminaries. The precipitate decline of vocations, the absence of either theory or data collection in seminary planning, and the restless quest to try something new every year do not seem likely to change in the immediate future. If there is to be any progress at all in developing new theories of the training of priests, I suspect the direction will come from forces outside the seminary system.

5. Dating

One of the major criticisms of the seminary system of old was that the rule against social interaction with women inhibited the emotional maturation of the future clergy. The rule against dating, in whatever seminaries in which it still might be on the books, is sufficiently a dead letter at the present, and it need not concern us. Whether there is any greater maturity among seminarians now than in the past is a question which in the present state of the research we cannot answer. However, there is no evidence that teen-age dating or the lack thereof had any impact on the adult attitudes and behavior of the priests we studied. Their emotional maturity, as we shall discuss in the next chapter, is not much different from that of the typical American male. What this suggests is not so much that priests are heterosexually mature as that they are no more immature than are typical American males—a thought which may be more of a reflection on the state of the evolution of the species than it is a positive comment on the priesthood.

I do not disagree with what some psychological theorists say about the contribution of heterosexual relationships to the maturation process of the late adolescent male. I am prepared to believe that some sort of meaningful intimacy with a woman of his own age can be an immense contribution to the personality development of a young man (and vice versa, of course). What I am skeptical about is how many young men are fortunate enough to have such relationships. Given the pecking order of the mating, dating game and the something less than adequate preparation for adult sexuality that is typical of American child rearing, one ought not to be surprised that healthy growth-producing relationships in later stages of adolescence are quite infrequent.

I am not suggesting that young people, either seminarians or not, should not try for such relationships. I only suggest that the mythology widely prevalent in some areas about the indispensability of such relationships in the quest for personal maturity needs to be viewed with skepticism; and the corresponding fiction that priests are more inept than most males in dealing with women also ought to be abandoned. As one married woman theologian puts it, "What makes them think that married men know how to deal with women?"

RECOMMENDATIONS

1. All those responsible for shaping thought and opinion in the Church should face the reality that the immigrant experience and the pre-Conciliar experience are likely to linger with us for the next several decades.

2. Similarly, we must also resign ourselves to the fact that ambiguity and confusion are likely to be with us as long as any of the readers of this book are still alive.

3. The clergy must realize that their rate of transition is likely to be much more rapid than that of most of their parishioners, that no useful purpose is served by attempting to shock or to force the laity into movement more rapidly than they are capable of. Nor is any useful purpose served by assuming that a priest can redefine the function of his role by himself without ongoing consultation with his people—all of his people, not just those who write letters to the editor of the *National Catholic Reporter*.

4. Priests must face the fact that mostly due to the new black insistence on cultural pluralism, the subject of ethnic groups is once again of critical importance in American society, especially to that organization of which there is none more ethnic, the Roman Church.

5. A major reappraisal is needed of the purposes and functions of seminaries and priestly training, a reappraisal that will not terminate in the issuance of yet another set of supposedly permanent episcopal guidelines. It might be advisable for a national commission to be established to sponsor long-term research, experimentation, and thought about the goals of priestly training. This commission would be heterogeneous in its membership like presidential commissions in this country or royal

commissions in England, though hopefully its findings would be taken more seriously than those of the presidential commissions. The business of training priests is too important to be left to seminary faculties and administrators. It is also too important to be left to seminarians, bishops, seminarian faculties, and administrators. All obviously have important input to make in redesigning the method of priestly training, but they certainly have no monopoly on concern over the outcome of such redesigning efforts.

I don't think such a commission will be set up, but if it is, I would like to go on record as saying that NORC would be only too happy to do research for it.

6. While I do not have any particular thoughts at the present about how the training of future clergy ought to be organized, much less about what curriculum it ought to involve, it seems to me that the following three goals are essential:

(a) The priest must be a man of intelligence, that is to say, he must be able to evaluate and choose between alternatives and to express his ideas in communication toward consensus (to use a formulation of Joseph Schwab, Professor of education at the University of Chicago). There is no substitute for intelligence in any kind of human endeavor, but in particular during a time of crisis, transition, and dramatic change, a man who cannot intelligently weigh alternatives before choosing and adequately communicate his ideas to others is a great liability to any organization he serves. It may be argued that most American college graduates are sadly deficient in both these abilities. I will not dispute the argument, but simply assert that quite independent of what most college graduates can do, priests must still be men of intelligence.

Some seminary faculty have responded to this idea by saying that the students simply are no longer interested in ideas, that they are only concerned with "creating community" and "rendering service." Both "community" and "service" are in fact ideas—if they are not meaningless slogans. I am not so sure

that seminarians or indeed young people in general are all that
unconcerned with ideas, but even if what the seminary faculty
says is true, then that is a misfortune for students, for either
they must become concerned about ideas or there should be
no place for them in the priesthood. Thomas Kempis was
wrong when he said that he would rather be able to feel
compunction than to define it, and so the modern seminarian
is wrong when he says he would rather be able to feel community than define it. If he does not understand what
community is with all its complexities and risks, he will be
inadequate and quite possibly dangerous as a community builder.
Man, of course, is not pure intellect, and the education of the
past, whether in the seminary or the college, which so emphasized the intellect so as to exclude the rest of man was
clearly inadequate. But the inadequacies of the past do not
justify our going to the other extreme in the present, and
if education without emotion is incomplete, so education without passionate concern for intellectual growth and development
is something less than human. I am sorry if young seminarians
are not concerned with things of the intellect; but they had
better become concerned with them or seek some other "meaningful" form of social service. Ideas are indispensable in the
modern world; they are, I think especially indispensable for
the clergy. Most of the problems of the Roman Church in the
United States today would not exist if twenty, thirty, forty
years ago there were more seminarians who were concerned
with ideas. The man of enthusiasm without ideas will never
transcend the enthusiasms of his own youth. It may be hard
for the young seminarians of today to believe it, but the most
reactionary of the elder clergy are as enthusiastic today as they
were when they were seminarians—and about the same things.
Enthusiasm, in other words, is no guarantee of intellectual or
human growth, but intellectual openness and curiosity is, if
not a guarantee, at least an absolutely essential prerequisite.

   (b) The priest-to-be must be a man of conviction; that is to

say, he must be committed to the message that he is supposed
to preach. I do not mean that he should be committed necessarily to certain dogmatic formulations of that message, because dogmatic formularies can and must change. He must be
convinced by the symbolism of the Real contained in the
New Testament of a God who is passionately, madly in love
with His people. It is a normal and healthy part of maturation for a young person to re-examine the worth of his religious
symbolism—though it seems to me that there is a tendency
in our time to prolong the time of religious doubt and hesitancy
beyond reasonable length in order that one may savor its full
and delicious delights. It is also true that one can never stop
going to the depths of understanding of the implications of
one's religious symbolism. It is also true, I think, that the pose
of perpetual doubt which is so beloved by certain Catholic
intellectuals at the present time is psychologically extremely unhealthy. One must eventually take a stand; one must make a leap
of faith either for or against the fundamental graciousness of
Being. Until one makes one's leap in either direction, one is
psychologically and religiously immature. The young man who
approaches ordination without having made that fundamental
leap simply should not be ordained, I am very sorry to say.
One hopes that he will work out his religious problems, but
he ought not to be permitted to work them out by imposing
his confusions, doubts, and anxieties on the people for whom
he is supposed to be a religious leader. He should be disabused
of the notion that the posture of permanent doubt is a sign
of openness or maturity; it is rather a sign that religiously one
is still adolescent, quite incapable of making a decisive commitment one way or the other.

Secular humanism is admirable; social reform is praiseworthy;
radical posturing may be tolerable at least and in some cases
obligatory; psychotherapeutic skills are useful and on occasion
indispensable. All of these may be legitimate consequences of
religious conviction and commitment, but they are not sub-

stitutes for it. The young man who thinks they are, whatever other admirable merits he may have, simply ought not to be made a priest.

(c) Finally, a future priest should be a man of prayer—an assertion which surely makes more clear than anything else possibly could what a square I am. Nevertheless, the resurgence of interest in the occult and the mystical on the secular university campus is proof, if any were needed, that an attempt to establish some kind of harmony with the fundamental forces of the universe is an indispensable and probably permanent need of the human personality. Furthermore, he who is unable to wrench himself away from the obligations of the everyday world to reflect upon his goals, destiny, and purpose is going to become something less than human very quickly. Prayer, or something that is its functional equivalent, is of necessity for a fully human life. Social action and group discussion, while they may be important inputs of the contemplative process, are not an adequate substitute for it. If all men should be men of prayer, it seems to me to be especially required for clergymen whose words and deeds are expected to symbolize and to make incarnate for others the conviction about and commitment to the message he proclaims. If a young man does not want to live in such a way that his person symbolizes a certain kind of religious conviction, then I am sorry, but however admirable he may be in other respects, he has no business trying to be a priest.

There is no aspect of the current identity of crisis of the Roman Church in the United States that is more distressing than the pathetic quest for "relevance"—and relevance is usually defined by the headlines of the day before yesterday. One can hear it said that intelligence, conviction, and prayerfulness (qualities I consider essential to be a priest) are irrelevant for a modern world. I am rather inclined to doubt it—and I would remind the reader that I am far more part of the secular modern world than are most priests or, indeed, most Catholic laity, for that matter. On the contrary, I am persuaded that intelligence, conviction, and prayerfulness are probably more relevant than they ever were. But the point is not whether they are relevant; it is whether they are valid. I do not think we can now, any more than at any previous time in history, conclude the validity of human postures by counting noses. As my friend Peter Berger says of the possibility that religion is outmoded in the modern world, "so much the worse for the modern world; it will pass, but religion will not."

2

EMOTIONAL MATURITY

Simultaneous with the NORC research, a team at the psychology department of Loyola University under the direction of Eugene C. Kennedy was doing a psychological study of a smaller sample of priests. Presumably, anyone interested in a detailed consideration of the emotional maturity of the clergy will wish to read this study. However, as a complement to the personality study, a personality test—recommended by the Loyola staff—was administered to one quarter of the six thousand priests in the NORC study. The test, called the POI (Personality Orientation Inventory), was devised by Professor Everett Shostrom to operationally measure the self-actualizing notions of Professor Abraham Maslow. Briefly, the self-actualized person is neither hyperindependent nor hypoindependent; that is to say, he is able to occupy a middle ground between being excessively dependent on others and excessively independent of them. The self-actualizing person is "interested in developing and utilizing all of his unique capabilities or potentialities free of the inhibitions and emotional turmoils of those less self-actualized." The self-actualized person "is able to tie the past and the future to the present into meaningful continuity," and "he goes through life apparently independent but still obeying his internal piloting . . . The source of direction for the individual is inner in the sense that he is guided by internal motivations rather than external influences."

FINDINGS

A detailed discussion of the scores of priests on the POI scales, and the comparison between them and other groups can be found in Chapter Four of *American Priests*. The principal findings, however, may be summarized as follows:

1. There are no appreciable differences between priests and people in their own age category on measures of self-actualization. The young priests, for example, score higher on the self-actualization scales than college students, and compare favorably with Peace Corps volunteers.[1]

2. There is a slight relationship between an "inner-directed" personality score and a propensity to resign from the priesthood. However, it appears that there is a tendency for resignees to be hyperactualized, and for those who remain to be hypoactualized. In other words, some of those who leave the priesthood show excessive needs for independence, and some of those who stay show excessive needs for dependence, which suggests that some men leave because they are overactualized and some men stay because they are underactualized. It must be noted, however, that the overwhelming majority of those who score high on the self-actualization measures remain in the priesthood.

3. Nor is there any evidence for the frequent assertion that priests have passive-dependent personalities. The indication is that one of the principal emotional deficiencies of priests is a slight tendency to be less able than others to cope with aggressive feelings; in other words, the priest is, if anything, more

---

[1] Unfortunately, practically no research has been done on the self-actualization scores of people over forty; thus comparisons are limited to priests under forty. Among priests there seems to be a negative correlation between age and self-actualization; that is to say, the older one gets, the lower the self-actualization score. Dr. Shostrom and his colleagues have no data available to indicate whether this negative correlation would exist in the general population, though in consultation with the NORC staff, Shostrom remarked that he thought such a negative correlation was likely.

passive-aggressive than passive-dependent. If he has any tendency in passive directions it is to control others by his passivity. His neurotic style, when it exists, is more likely to be that of the "nice guy" rather than that of the dependent child.

4. There are also some indications of special strengths in the priesthood. It would appear that priests are relatively stronger than other groups in their ability to affirm their own self-worth and to accept themselves for what they are in spite of weaknesses and deficiencies.

5. There is no indication that those who entered the seminary later or who had more postordination educational experience score any higher on measures of self-actualization than do other priests.

6. Neither is there any evidence to indicate that the clergy are any more deficient than comparable groups in their capacity for intimate friendships.

7. Finally, there is no evidence at all that the priesthood has attracted men whose social class family background or childhood experiences have made them less likely to be autonomous than the typical American male.

SPECULATIONS

1. Most of the findings on the personality inventory were negative. Priests are not emotionally deficient, at least not when compared with other American males. There is no grounds in our data either for self-pity on the part of priests or that sort of paralyzing "you poor man, what terrible things they did to you" sympathy that certain Catholic laity seem only too willing to offer the clergy. (One suspects it is a subtle form of anti-clericalism which seeks to reverse the role relationships that these laity knew in childhood.) This is not to say that no cruel or unjust things were done to young men in seminaries or to priests, young, middle-aged, and old, in the ministry. Severe injuries were inflicted, severe harm was done, but most

priests managed to survive it—at least as well as other American males survived the injuries and harm done to them, and at least as well as we all survived the most serious traumas of all, those of early childhood. Man is a remarkably resilient creature, and the rigid authoritarianism of both the seminary and the parish did not apparently destroy the resiliency of most priests. It did not even seem to impede their capacity to grow any more than the socialization of other American males impeded their capacity to grow.

To say that no more serious harm was done to priests than was done to other American males is to say something important; but from one point of view it is to say something not all that important. If the Church as an organizational structure is no more repressive than the rest of society, it is scarcely an accomplishment to be proud of, and while we can breathe something of a sigh of relief with evidence that the seminary did not destroy the powers of self-actualization of the men who went through it, such accomplishment is, after all, meager. One would have expected that from a community that claims to be what the Church claims to be, a seminary training would have produced a more self-actualized person. Granted that the role of a clergyman as a bureaucratic functionary did not call for self-actualization, granted even more that self-actualization was certainly viewed by some in official positions in the Church (though scarcely using the word) as organizationally dysfunctional, it is still a miserable failure of a community that claims to be Christian when the best it can say of its men who are to serve as its leaders and symbolize by their words and deeds the words of Jesus that they are really not inferior to anyone else.

2. The feeling that many priests seem to have that their emotional development somehow or other is less impressive than that of other American males is largely the result of the grass looking greener in someone else's socialization experience—perhaps also the result of a gross idealization of the

maturational importance of the marriage relationship for most men. There is never reason, of course, for any of us to assume that we are paragons of emotional maturity, nor that there is no longer any need for emotional growth; but a motivation for personality development and expansion that is based on a feeling that one is inferior to others is, in addition to being of dubious effectiveness, simply not in accord with the facts. There are some priests, including those who have ventured into print in recent years, who feel a desperate need to prove to themselves that they are men. There is also a natural tendency for those priests, and for all priests, to blame their personality weaknesses on the Church. However, realistically, they should realize that their inadequate sense of their own manhood is rooted in experiences much earlier in their lives than their decisions to enter the seminary or their experiences in the priesthood. It is a weakness they have in common with many who are not priests. The Church, the seminary, the bishop, our superior, our pastor—they are all superb scapegoats on which we can blame our personality problems. In a negative sense, perhaps some of that blame is proper; after all, none of them did anything much to facilitate our emotional growth. But our problems are fundamentally within us, and while they may have been aggravated and reinforced somewhat by the ec- clesiastical structure, their causes are to be found elsewhere. Furthermore, there is no evidence that the Church as structure aggravates personality problems more than any other organiza- tional structure in contemporary society.

3. The strengths found in the personalities of priests—es- pecially the ability to assert their self-worth in the face of weaknesses and difficulties and the inclination to take a con- structive view of the nature of man—are probably not surprising in men who chose the vocation in which they deal explicitly with religion. If the priest is slightly more optimistic about both himself and other men, one ought not to be especially surprised; only one with a dash of optimism would get into

a profession in which most of his dealings must be with people. Obviously we are not saying that all priests are optimists, rather, we only say that there is some tendency for priests to be more optimistic about themselves and about man than are other American males. But while this additional optimism may not be very great, it is nonetheless not an asset to be lightly dismissed. It may even explain to some extent why morale of the clergy continues to be rather good despite the turbulence and confusion of the present critical period. To put the matter somewhat differently: If priests frequently feel discouraged, they have some reason now for thinking that other people may feel even more discouraged than they do.

4. Furthermore, the tendency to be passive-aggressive, that is to say, to control people not so much by self-assertion as by being "a nice guy," is not especially surprising considering the fact that the priestly role until recently was one in which a man had many and serious responsibilities with rather little authority and independence to meet them. Given the absolute control of bishop over pastor, of pastor over priest, superior over subject, the dependent person in the dyad obtains sufficient emotional space both to deal with his superior and his client not by self-assertion, not by releasing his aggressive feelings, not by sharply and vigorously defining limitations of self beyond which no man dare trespass, but rather by charming them— much the way the altar boy charmed the crusty old pastor. One of the emotional problems of the priests at the present time is that for a number of different reasons it is now not only possible but in some instances necessary to release one's aggressive feelings, to begin asserting one's selfhood, and to initiate the process of drawing lines which others may not cross. It is very hard to learn how to do this in the later years of life. When the passive-aggressive personality begins to assert his aggressiveness overtly, he is likely to exaggerate considerably the cathartic behavior, and of course he has a lot of past aggressions to release, aggressions both toward his superiors

and teachers from the past as well as those from his childhood that he has never properly faced. One wonders how much of the conflict in the present milieu of American Catholicism is a part of the painful process of "nice guys" trying to become effective militants. Too bad more of them didn't have some experience as precinct captains.

5. The psychologists with whom we consulted about the use of the Personality Orientation Inventory were impressed with the "euphoria" or the "binge of health" or the "excessive independence" demonstrated by the scores of many of the resigned priests whom we surveyed. I found myself much less surprised by this. It is clear both from analysis and my own impression that many (though obviously by no means all) priests who resigned were extremely unhappy in the priesthood, and that the decision to resign was an extraordinarily difficult one made at the price of great emotional stress and anxiety. Once that decision was made and they had definitely undertaken to depart from a situation which was increasingly intolerable, a tremendous feeling of euphoria was bound to occur. The euphoria will certainly not persist, but whether, as Jesuit psychiatrist James Gill has suggested, the emotional problems will return in the years after resignation is a moot point. In a later chapter we will make some comments on the subject. It is necessary to emphasize, however, even in this chapter, that the preliminary evidence shows that those who left the priesthood were deeply unhappy in it. This may seem to be an obvious enough point, for if one is happy as a priest, why would he leave? Nonetheless, it is a point which does not seem to be self-evident in much of the current discussion concerning the priesthood.

6. Perhaps the most important point to be stressed in this chapter is that the POI scores of priests indicate that they are by and large men who have the kind of qualities required to be clergymen in the immigrant Tridentine Church. They are not strongly self-actualized but neither are they deficient in

personality development when compared to other Americans. They are not strongly self-assertive and do not display much capacity to deal with their own aggressive feelings; on the other hand, they are hopeful about both themselves and the human condition—precisely those qualities required of those who are to be cultic and social service functionaries in what is essentially a static, inward-looking, and defensive ecclesiastical organization. To what extent such characteristics were inculcated in priests through their training, and to what extent there was a selective recruitment in which only men with such characteristics found the priesthood attractive is far too complicated to be dealt with even in an elaborate research project such as the one we are reflecting on. My own inclination is to feel some skepticism about the ability of secondary and higher educational institutions to change personalities. I think men were attracted to the priesthood precisely because they saw in it an outlet for their own personality strengths and a protection from their personality weaknesses.

There is not much in the personality scores we are discussing in this chapter to indicate that there is a strong streak of the prophetic in American priests, but then the way the American Church was organized until 1960 left little room for the prophetic. The problem of the present may well be not so much that priests have low self-actualizing scores as that in the present state of things the Church needs far more strongly self-actualized clergymen than it has now. In the future, hopefully, men motivated much more by internal conviction than by external constraints will be attracted to the priesthood. However, it is important to note that the most important way to attract such men to the priesthood is to define both the role and the training of priests in such a way that strong personalities are attracted to it. Modifications of the training experience ought to be designed not with the view of turning potential "nice guys" into self-actualizers—a difficult and dubious task at best—but rather in attracting those who are self-actualizers in the first place.

7. As will be reported in later chapters, priests by and large seem to have survived the traumatic crises of the 1960s with a good deal of vigor and resilience, but all this statement indicates is that on the average, priests have proved strong enough to sustain the pressures of the present moment. For many, including some who have left (though obviously not all), the strain is extremely difficult and painful. Many priests have been able to respond to the challenge of the very new situation in which they find themselves in such a way as to make important developmental progress, though I doubt that for anyone it has been particularly easy. But other priests find it difficult if not impossible to make such emotional progress by themselves, and still others find themselves caught in a state of fear and anxiety which, if it is no worse than that which faces lay people, is nonetheless demoralizing. It is clear, I think, that many of us need some form of growth-facilitating experience. It would be appropriate for ecclesiastical authorities to make such experiences either in group or individual counseling situations widely available for priests, without any stigma attached to those who avail themselves of such services. On the other hand, the rank amateurism of many self-licensed practitioners of therapy is likely to do far more harm than good. I think that much of the training of professional therapists, be they psychologists or psychiatrists, is even more ritualistic and meaningless than the training of the clergy in the seminaries of yesteryear, and it is quite possible that some gifted amateur without such training but some special quality of sensitivity and/or experience with a skilled supervisor may be a more effective therapist than the man with a wall lined with sheepskin diplomas. Though some amateurs may indeed be more effective than some professionals, I think the presumption ought normally to be the contrary. The possessor of an M.A. in counseling and guidance from an education school who sets himself up as a prac-

titioner of group therapy ought to be viewed with serious reservations. Unfortunately, the same immigrant anti-intellectualism that made it inevitable for the Church never to encourage the development of the historians, social scientists, and theologians it needed to cope with the present crisis also guaranteed that it would not have available anywhere near the number of trained therapists it needs. The same genius for the ad hoc, penny-wise, pound-foolish response that characterized seminary reform as described in the last chapter devised the strategy for training therapists: The assumption has been that a half-trained therapist is better than no therapist, which is like saying that a half-trained surgeon is half as good as a fully trained one.

RECOMMENDATIONS

1. It is time that everyone in the Church, laity, clergy, public spokesmen, private citizen, stop scapegoating the Church for emotional problems. As the lady theologian quoted in a previous chapter once remarked to me,[2] "I often wonder what would have happened to a lot of people if Pope Paul had approved birth control. What would they blame then for the failures of their marriages?" It is perfectly legitimate to insist that certain aspects of the structures and doctrinal formulations of the Church did absolutely nothing to facilitate our emotional growth and may well have reinforced the negative elements in our personalities that stood in the way of such growth; but most of the limitations we experience in personal development are those we had long before we came into contact with the institutional Church. One of the surest signs of the beginning of emotional growth is the elimination of the need to use the Church as scapegoat. In other words, it is a sign of wisdom to realize that the Church cultural structures are much more likely to be an effect rather than a cause of something deeper and more profound within the tradition of which we were a part. The self-

[2] To put a lot of suspicious minds at rest, the lady theologian is my sister.

hatred and inability to express emotion of so many Irish males
—and the consequent proclivity to alcoholism—can scarcely be
blamed on Catholicism, since there are other countries equally
Catholic where the problems are, if anything, just the opposite.
In both sets of circumstances what has happened is that a cultural
heritage has fastened upon an aspect of Catholicism that responds
to its own needs, and emphasized this aspect to the exclusion
of other rather different components of the Catholic tradition.
The ethos of American Catholicism will change not so much
when we get different bishops (though, heaven knows, different
bishops are necessary), nor when we get a married clergy
(though a married clergy may be a positive asset) but when we
who have created that ethos, unconsciously and implicitly, perhaps, are able to change ourselves. The ethos can be changed
only when we will be able to make a decisive enough break with
the past to change the socialization experience of a substantial
number of our young people during infancy, childhood, and
adolescence. Such an effort is, of course, a monumental task, and
it may take decades if not centuries to accomplish. Scapegoating
is much easier.

2. It is necessary for ecclesiastical leaders to begin to think
of ways in which the role and training of the priest can be
redefined in order to make the priesthood attractive for strong,
self-assertive, vigorous men (and women too, for that matter).
It must be conceded that such men, impatient, innovative,
vigorous, creative, do not make good bureaucrats, or good as-
sistant pastors, or good chancery office flunkies, or, for that
matter, docile bishops who belch when the apostolic delegate
has indigestion. However, one very much wonders whether if
Ignatius of Loyola, Vincent de Paul, Francis of Assisi, Robert
Bellarmine, or Philip Neri would have been attracted to the
seminary or the ministry if they were alive in our own time.
Most likely these gifted innovators would meet the same fate
today as they did in their own eras: They would be forced
to create their own counterinstitutions, since there is no room

for them in existing ones. One supposes that the leadership of the Church can sit by and hopefully expect the appearance of a modern equivalent of these innovators. One can even hope that ecclesiastical authorities will not follow the example of some of their predecessors and denounce such innovators on sight; but while it may be sound religion to expect the innovators, it is not good organizational practice to wait for them. Therefore, however difficult it may be and however unlikely the present hierarchy is to engage in such an endeavor, it is still of great importance that the redefinition of the priestly role stresses the priest as prophet rather more than the priest as functionary.

3. To make psychiatric services available to those who are considering leaving the priesthood is a legitimate exercise of one of the corporal-works of mercy. However, in terms of permitting an opportunity for such a person's emotional growth to occur while he remains in the priesthood, such psychiatric help is belated. By the time most potential resignees are willing to seek counseling, they are already caught in a psychological process in which they can only find peace and relief by the decisive act of resignation. Counseling may help them to understand the dimensions and implications of resignation, and facilitate their adjustment to the new life they are choosing. However, there are, if our data to be discussed in a later chapter are to be believed, somewhere between 80 and 90 per cent of the priests in the country who are not likely to resign. It will take a great deal of diplomacy to make counseling resources available to those who would profit from them in that 80 or 90 per cent. It will also require something of a miracle, since one looks in vain for anywhere near the number of counselors who might be needed. What is probably required is a long-range plan in which all clergymen feel not only free to seek psychiatric help but also view it as part of their own professional development, much as do good psychotherapists. Indeed, anyone who must deal with people at the levels of

intensity and duration required of a parish priest simply cannot expect to function at a high level of effectiveness unless he enjoys an ever increasing understanding of and control over his own emotional responses. Periodic counseling experiences may not be as necessary for a priest as they are for a therapist, but I would be at a loss to think of any other profession that needs such experiences more than the clergy.

3

THE SPIRITUALITY OF PRIESTS

FINDINGS

1. Priests still pray. Eighty-five per cent of them say Mass every day, 92 per cent of them feel that the Mass is a very important form of prayer and worship, 53 per cent read the Bible once a week or more, and 46 per cent of the diocesan priests (and 57 per cent of the religious) meditate each day.

2. Younger clergy are less likely to engage in some of the traditional forms of spirituality. Only 72 per cent of those under thirty-five say Mass every day, although 88 per cent of them consider the Mass to be an important form of worship. Only about two fifths pray privately every day, but three fifths—more than the average—read the Bible once a week or more. Whether these levels of priestly prayer are lower or higher than the levels achieved in the past is impossible to say in the absence of data from the past. The percentages of those practicing frequently the traditional forms of piety are somewhat lower than the ideal, but higher than one would expect in a situation where concern about the spiritual had vanished.

3. The Roman Breviary is in deep trouble. While 86 per cent of the bishops say it all every day, only 43 per cent of the priests do, and only 15 per cent of the clergy under thirty-five and 30 per cent of those between thirty-six and forty-five say it all every day. Only 1 per cent of the bishops report

saying it not at all, but 30 per cent of the active priests did, and 50 per cent of the priests under thirty-five.

4. Many priests report "mystical" or "quasi-mystical" experiences "frequently" during the past two or three years. Twenty-six per cent say they have had "an overwhelming feeling of being at one with God or Christ," 56 per cent say they have "a sense of being in the presence of God," and 47 per cent say they have "a deep feeling of being personally loved by Christ here and now." The proportions of those reporting such experiences are somewhat lower for those under thirty-five.

But the relationship between age and an index of religious experience is only .1, scarcely enough to take notice of, for only 1 per cent of the variants on the scale measuring religious experience can be explained by youthfulness.

5. The only other important correlate of religious experience is family tension. Those who came from tense family backgrounds (one where there was either tension between parents or between a parent and the respondent) are less likely to report that they have had religious experience. The negative correlation is not high (—.18), but given the very crude measures of both family tension and religious experience, the relationship is interesting.

6. There is also a relationship between prayer and religious experiences, but the modest .29 correlation between how often one prays and whether one experiences the presence of God means that a little less than 10 per cent of the variant on the "quality" of one's prayer can be explained by the "quantity" of that prayer. The traditional theological position that mysticism is a gift which cannot be directly pursued receives some confirmation from this finding.

SPECULATIONS

1. One of the most fascinating phenomena of the last decade has been the collapse of the obligation to say the Roman

Breviary. Although one hears that in European countries (of course with the exception of Mother Ireland) the obligation was taken much less seriously than it was in the United States, there is no doubt that until rather recently the obligation of reciting the Divine Office was one from which few American priests would excuse themselves even under the most difficult of circumstances. The car pulled over to the side of the road at night with the occupant reading vespers and compline by flashlight; the solitary figure separated from the rest of the party, poring over his black book; the Breviary recited while eyes moved from 118th Psalm to the television screen; the dinner guest who had to leave at ten o'clock because he still had all the Breviary to say were such familiar clerical figures one took them almost for granted. Their disappearance was abrupt and unexpected; though they may not have been missed, it was noted by everyone how quickly they departed. The change of attitude is even more startling when we recall that most of us were taught in the seminary that to miss even a substantial section of one hour of the Breviary was a serious sin for which a God who kept careful accounts of such things might easily commit us to eternal perdition. Looking back on such an idea, it is easy for us to realize how nonsensical it was; nonetheless, as long as it was supported by the rigid structure of the Counter Reformation Church, few people dared to question it, and in fact the obligation still remains on the books. When the questionnaire for the present study was being designed, some bishops were uneasy about even asking a question about the Breviary, since, they said, we might be asking a priest to "manifest his conscience," that is to say, to admit publicly that he had sinned.

It may be that the mistake made with the Breviary was to reform it; had it been kept in Latin and unintelligible, men might have gone on reciting it as a meaningless but sacred obligation. Once it was put into English, the absurdity of dashing through vast numbers of Psalms and obscure readings from the fathers was such that the credibility of the obligation could no longer be maintained. The collapse of the Breviary may well be an interesting example of a reform that was not drastic enough. Merely translating the Breviary into English destroyed the sense of obligation without providing any attractive alternative. More comprehensive Breviary reform (one hears it is still bottled up in the Roman Congregation) came too late; in fact, it has not yet come at all. When it does come, it may very well be that most priests will view it with grave skepticism, no matter how useful a form of prayer it may be. Threats from some religious leaders that the new Breviary will be binding under pain of sin[1] is not likely to impress priests very much.

At a more general level it can be said that obligatory prayer is effective in a rigid, tightly structured Church where all sorts of grave penalties can be invoked for those who do not pray, but in a fluid, changing Church, where man has lost his fear of penalties threatened by moral theology books or canon law commentaries, the obligation to pray "under pain of serious sin" has no force at all. Men who pray, if they do pray, do so because they want to or need to or like to, not because they are being forced to pray. Unfortunately, many of us will probably go through a period in which, childishly but understandably, we refuse to pray in order to protest against the absurdity of the compulsory prayer of the past.

2. We Americans are not a particularly mystical people, and nothing in the training of American Catholics, in their schools, their parishes, their seminaries, or their convents, in years gone by was likely to induce us to develop habits of prayer and mysticism. There were certain routine "spiritual exercises" that we were expected to carry out, but we did so with as much speed as possible in order to get on with our work, and like the good Protestants we were, we knew it was work that

[1] "Just like fast and abstinence," is what one ecclesiastic says—whatever in the world that means in the present state of things.

counted. There was no time to be playful, speculative, reflec-
tive, creative; under such circumstances, of course, there was
no time to be mystical or ecstatic. The real mystic or ecstatic
would have had a very hard time being ordained in American
seminaries of the past.

He would have an equally hard time now, though perhaps
for different reasons. Mysticism and ecstasy are simply impossible if one is unable to detach oneself from routine, mundane
responsibilities. There was indeed irony in all of this: Prayer
itself became a mundane, routine responsibility, and instead of
predisposing one for contemplative, mystical, ecstatic experience,
it was simply one more obstacle to it. It is surprising that
so many priests have some kind of experience of the presence
of God.

Yet I don't suppose there are many of us who feel guilty
about spending too much time in prayer. The older priest has
too much work to do to "waste" a lot of time praying, and
the younger priest is convinced that group discussion and social
action are the same things as prayer. Both men have strong
strains, one suspects, of the obsessive-compulsive about them,
and however useful it may be for getting things done, it is
not the stuff out of which mystics and ecstatics are made.

3. As a reaction to the rigid rituals of strict, obligatory
prayers of the past, there has been a tendency in the Church
for the last half decade toward a very low Church form of
worship, including even the "Marijuana Mass," whose glories I
celebrated in another book.[2] Partly as a rejection of past mistakes and partly out of a desire to be "with it" in the new
secular city, many of us bent every effort toward removing
all possible traces of the sacred, the ritual, the otherworldly,
and the transcendent from our worship, public or private.

Harvey Cox then made his pilgrimage from The Secular
City to The Feast of Fools, and mysticism and ecstasy were

[2] Andrew M. Greeley, *Come Blow Your Mind with Me* (Garden City,
N.Y., Doubleday & Company, Inc., 1971).

suddenly "in" again at Harvard Divinity School. Most of us are not nearly so agile as Professor Cox. While we occasionally do attempt to introduce some of the psychedelic into our liturgies, we are still afraid to be too sacred or too transcendent. One young priest I know once introduced a prayer at Mass, "Oh God, in whatever sense we believe in Him." It is ironic, of course, that just as we are abandoning the last vestiges of the mysterious and the transcendent in our worship, some young people are striving, frequently in bizarre ways, to re-create for themselves both contemplation and liturgy. The problem is that liturgy was not merely ritual, it was ritualized; and our contemplation was not free and spontaneous but compulsory. We are probably going to have to get out of our systems both the obligations and the ritualism of the past before we can catch up with the new quest for the sacred—and heaven only knows where Professor Cox will be by then.

4. One of the principal difficulties of obligatory religion is that it makes one intellectually sloppy. If one can be sure that the members of one's church will do what they are supposed to do out of a sense of obligation, one is less motivated to develop intellectually meaningful justifications for their behavior. Much of post-Tridentine immigrant Catholicism was based on unquestioned religious obligations. When suddenly and dramatically those obligations were questioned, there was not readily available a theoretical rationale which provided meaningful reasons for continuing the behavior now it was no longer thought to be obligatory.[3] Why say the Breviary? Why recite the Rosary? Why make retreats? Why engage in spiritual reading? Why meditate? The answer was easy. We did it because we were told to and because we had to. But those obligations no longer enjoy much credibility, and while there are excellent reasons for praying, no one seems to have had them available

[3] The problem of theoretical sloppiness based on unquestioned obligation is especially pertinent to the celibacy issue, as we shall see in a later chapter.

when the bottom fell out of obligatory prayer five years ago. It might not have mattered much if the justifications were available because it was probably inevitable that there would be a period of violent reaction against anything that was once imposed under obligation. What will happen, then, is that the good things which lost their vitality because they were compulsory will have to be rediscovered. Unfortunately, it may take a long time.

5. And yet there are some signs of change. A number of seminary professors have told me, some with obvious surprise, that there are young men under their tutelage who actually pray on their own; indeed, they do such things as going off to Trappist monasteries for whole weeks to pray—an option that was not available to seminarians in my day, not that many of us would have thought seriously of doing it if we could. I was further assured that such young men were not creepy or stupid, but some of the best in their classes. Prayer has been around for a long time, and, as I suggested earlier, it is unlikely that the human proclivity for mysticism and ecstasy has vanished. (Professor Cox certainly rediscovered it quickly enough.) However, if prayer is to be rediscovered by the Roman Catholic Church, or at least its clergy, it may very well be that it will be rediscovered under the leadership of young men like those seminarians who for some unaccountable reason seemed to want to pray even though they don't have to.

RECOMMENDATIONS

1. We all ought to pray more. (And I include myself in that obligation.)

2. We all ought to meditate and reflect more.

3. The Church ought to make available for priests periods of time—days, weeks, if necessary even a year—which can be devoted to prayer and reflection. This may be an odd state-

ment, because the annual retreat is still on the books as a matter of obligation—though one suspects that as an obligation it is no more effective than the obligation of the Breviary. What I am suggesting, however, is that an effective strategy might be to eliminate officially obligations for prayer and reflection and make available as a matter of right and privilege the time to pray and reflect for those who desire it. Attendance at retreat houses may decline, though heaven knows it is declining in any case, but at least those who attended would be there because they are exercising a privilege and a right, not because they are under constraint. Over the long haul, I suspect that attendance might increase. However, our optimistic conviction that good habits can be developed by compulsion (as manifested by those long, foolish lines of children herded into the confessional on the Thursday before First Friday) makes it very difficult for many of us to cope with the idea that reflection and contemplation are a privilege rather than an obligation.

The compromise we arrive at is to say that a priest can fulfill his obligation to make a retreat by participating in a "study week." Now study weeks are admirable events—suitable for fun and games, change of scenery, dalliance, for some, the beginnings of courtship, and for some, even learning something (though one can't learn much in a week, no matter how brilliant the speakers); but whatever else it is, it is not a time of reflection, prayer, and contemplation. The clergy certainly should be free, indeed encouraged, to improve their understanding and skills, but to confuse a study week with a week of prayerful reflection shows that one does not understand what either activity really is.

4. What I would like to see is a revival of ascetical and mystical theology. As the organization which presides over the oldest tradition of mysticism in the Western world, one would have thought that the Roman Church would have been delighted at the prospect of enriching this tradition by initiating

a dialogue between ascetical theology and modern psychology and sociology. But somehow or other that opportunity, like so many other comparable ones, thus far seems to be overlooked. I suppose that only if a sufficient number of priests and bishops are persuaded that contemplation is really important and is really something much more sophisticated than kneeling in church and fingering beads,[4] only then will ascetical theology be seen as something important. Now, alas, it is quickly and easily dismissed as being irrelevant. Obviously, people like John of Ruysbroeck, Meister Eckhardt, John of the Cross, and Teresa of Avila are luxuries and not necessities.

5. I should also like to see a greater willingness on the part of the clergy to listen to the laity who have contemplative or prayerful instincts. I have grave reservations about the Catholic Pentecostal movement; but there is no doubt in my mind that part of its strength is that it provides lay people with an opportunity to pray. Obviously not all laity, perhaps not even a majority, want to pray, at least very frequently; and yet it would seem to me that there are those with an authentic inclination who could be very important people in a Christian community. Priests should seek them out, encourage them, and perhaps (God save us) even learn from them.

6. Finally, I should hope that religious priests would engage in major efforts to rethink the meaning of the religious life, and particularly the role of prayer and contemplation in the religious community. I cannot believe that a form of human association which has met fundamental needs for a millennium and a half and more is going to go out of existence; but I do wish that someone would rethink what the religious life basically means. I am very much impressed by most of the young Jesuits I know, but I must confess the theoretical explication I read of "what a new Jesuit is" seems to me to be something less than satisfactory. The rhetoric of St. Ignatius

---

[4] Though I do not want to deny that for some people such activity was and still may be valid and meaningful religious behavior.

of Loyola may be out of fashion in our day, but I am not convinced that his fundamental religious insight is out of fashion at all, and his rules for the discernment of spirits strike me as being especially appropriate for our time. If young Jesuits want to burn draft files or applaud those that do, that is, I guess, their business, though such behavior strikes me as being politically counterproductive; but I would like to think that there is more to being a Jesuit or a Dominican or a Franciscan or a Vincentian in our day and age than that. I am sure there is, and I would hope that someone will rather quickly articulate what that means—and then stay in the priesthood long enough to live it. (Unlike one theoretician of the "new Jesuits" who left the Jesuits to get marrried shortly after he described what he and his fellows were like.)

There is, I am certain, a possibility of reformulating the rationale for the religious life which would make it pertinent and meaningful and relevant (though not in the narrow modern sense of that word) for our time. It would be inappropriate, however, for a diocesan priest to engage in such a reformulation.

It's hard enough trying to figure out where a diocesan priest should be.

4

SEXUALITY

FINDINGS

1. Only 40 per cent of the priests in the country still support the Church's official teaching on birth control. Eighty-three per cent of the bishops do as opposed to 13 per cent of the priests under thirty-five (and 30 per cent of those between thirty-six and forty-five).

2. Thirteen per cent of the priests in the country still say that they would refuse absolution to a penitent who had not promised to give up contraceptives, and 33 per cent more say that while they would discourage the use of artificial contraception, they would not deny absolution to a penitent on these grounds. The rest of the priests would leave the judgment on contraception to penitents themselves. While 13 per cent of all priests would refuse absolution, only 3 per cent of those under thirty-five and 8 per cent of those between thirty-six and forty-five would refuse absolution. Forty-two per cent of the bishops, however, would refuse absolution.

3. In the wake of the encyclical letter *Humanae Vitae*, 30 per cent of the priests in the country have changed their position with respect to birth control. Three per cent became more "conservative" and 27 per cent became more "liberal."

4. Thirty-three per cent have changed their confessional

procedure since the time of the encyclical, with 4 per cent becoming more conservative and 29 per cent more liberal.

5. Thirty-six per cent of the priests of the country thought that *Humanae Vitae* was a competent and appropriate use of papal teaching, 18 per cent more thought that the pope was within his authority to issue the encyclical, but that it was said at an inappropriate time. Thirty-three per cent more argued that *Humanae Vitae* was a misuse of authority because the pope failed to act with sufficient collegiality, and 9 per cent asserted that the pope was incompetent to teach in the area of birth control. Fourteen per cent of those under thirty-five thought that *Humanae Vitae* was a competent use of authority, as did 23 per cent of those between thirty-six and forty-five. However, 72 per cent of the bishops thought that it was a competent use of authority.

6. Only 29 per cent of the priests in the country are willing to say that adolescent masturbation is in most cases a serious sin.

7. Eighty per cent of the priests in the country think that premarital sex is morally unacceptable.

8. Only one third of the priests (but 58 per cent of the bishops) think that divorce in a marriage *ratum et consummatum* is forbidden by divine law and never can be permitted by the Church. While only 9 per cent of the priests think that in certain cases abortion may be morally permissible, another 40 per cent think that the Church has to allow "an open investigation of the issue."

SPECULATIONS

1. There isn't much doubt on the basis of the findings reported in the previous section that the traditional sexual teachings of the Catholic Church are in serious, probably fatal, trouble. Despite the steady stream of warnings issued by Rome and the national hierarchy, the majority of American clergy

no longer are willing to concede credibility to the Church's official position on birth control, divorce, and masturbation. It does not follow, however, that the clergy do not believe in any sexual morality, since the very large majority still reject both abortion and premarital sex. While we do not know what priests would have said on the subjects of birth control and divorce in 1960, we do know, at least in so far as a retrospective question can tell us, that about one quarter of the priests in the country have moved to the left on both birth control theory and birth control procedure in the confessional since the issuance of *Humanae Vitae*. This is an extraordinarily dramatic change, especially considering the prohibition against artificial birth control was the central concern of the American Church as far as practical catechetics was concerned. It was the one most frequently emphasized in sermons, books, classroom instruction, retreats, Cana conferences, pre-Cana conferences, and confessional counseling. In less than a half decade the majority has swung away from support of this central moral position to a refusal to try to enforce it. It may be one of the most dramatic shifts in the entire history of human ethics.

In addition, while the position one takes on birth control correlates with age, the shift in position does not; it seems to have occurred among all age groups of the clerical population. It is not merely the young clergy who are turning away from traditional sexual morality; all clergy are. The only exceptions seem to be the bishops, and our data make it clear that at the present time they enjoy no more credibility on this subject than does Rome.

It seems likely that we have here one more case of what happens to an obligation that is imposed by sheer authority at a time when the right of authority to impose obligations without supporting creditable justification is called into question. Once it became legitimate to question and change any of the rigid obligations of the post-Tridentine Church, it was inevitable that *all* the obligations would be questioned, and if adequate rationale was not advanced for them, they, too, would be changed, if not officially at least in the practical lives of Catholics. The fine distinctions that theologians and canonists would make between meat on Friday and the Latin Mass on the one hand and birth control and ecclesiastical celibacy on the other would escape not only most of the Catholic people but, as it turns out, most of the clergy too. Wise ecclesiastical authority, once it determined to make changes, would have realized that everything it had imposed in terms of pure authoritative obligation would be called into question; it would have been prepared to re-examine the rationale behind all its obligations. Unfortunately, ecclesiastical authority was not wise enough to anticipate such a crisis, and ethical theoreticians, like ascetical theoreticians, had grown sloppy. Since people could be expected to keep the Church's sexual regulations merely because of the assertion that they were also God's sexual regulations, it was not necessary for theoreticians to constantly re-examine the rationale for moral obligations. It was sufficient that people did what they were supposed to do without understanding why. Indeed, it was sufficient in a Church where nothing changed and nothing was under question, but it was not sufficient in a Church where everything was changing and everything was under question.

The encyclical *Humanae Vitae* was for all practical purposes an appeal to pure authority, a pure authority which the pope mistakenly assumed that he still had. The pope did list the arguments in favor of contraception, but he did not even bother to propound an intellectual response to them; he, in effect, dismissed them, and reasserted the prohibition against birth control couched entirely in terms of its being a prohibition based on "God's law." It is precisely here that the differences between the pope and the majority of priests and laity seem to exist. Many people simply do not believe any longer that such a prohibition is part of the divine law, and they do not believe the pope in terms of pure authority can say that it is.

The question immediately arises—and it did on the floor of the bishops' meeting when we made our presentation of the basic findings of the research project—that if priests still believe in God and the Church, how can they reconcile their faith with a rejection of papal authority on a matter so important? By the logic of the old formulation, such a rejection may indeed be inconsistent; but the point is that the logic of the old formulations is no longer accepted. Those priests and laity who reject the birth control teaching simply refuse to believe that they are rejecting something that is of the essence of either Christianity or Catholicism. In effect, what they are rejecting is the papal claim to be the uniquely authentic interpreter of Christianity on the point of birth control. They are not, in their own terms at least, rejecting Christianity, but they are rejecting a misunderstanding or misinterpretation of it. The pope, in other words, has made a serious, indeed tragic mistake, and they are not going to be bound by his mistakes.

It is not my purpose to repeat the arguments in favor of a change in the birth control position. It is clear that the fundamental weakness of the official stance is that it has proved incapable of taking into account either the massive world population problem or the development of sexual personalism that has occurred in the wake of the dramatic new insights of depth psychology. The official teaching is still caught in a mentality of population shortage, in the physical mechanics of procreation instead of the psychic dynamics of human love, in the authoritarian structure of the peasant family instead of the democratic structure of the modern urban family. The world of the official birth control position is one of the eighteenth century. While fundamental morality does not change with the centuries, the human context of moral behavior does. The fundamental theme of Catholic sexual morality is a respect for life; it is an important theme, desperately needed in the modern world, but it has been caught in certain rigid formulations, which not only obscure its basic content but seem to outsiders to represent the opposite of a concern for life. The negative prohibitions of the official sexual morality could be maintained only by the overwhelming force of a rigid, static authoritarian Church. As soon as that post-Tridentine ecclesiastical organization began to collapse, the credibility of the official sexual teaching evanesced, and Catholic moralists were completely unprepared to provide either a new rationale for the old ethic or a new line of development by which the old ethic could grow and transform itself. If Paul VI relied on sheer, naked authority in *Humanae Vitae*, only part of the explanation is that he unwisely thought he still possessed such authority. The rest of the explanation is that there was nothing else for him to do. He was unable to advance any solid arguments against change (and indeed against the majority of his own birth control commission) because he didn't have any such arguments. And neither did anyone else.

2. No matter how one wishes to view the situation, the encyclical *Humanae Vitae* was an ill-advised disaster. But there is no point repeating in this book the sad story of how the Roman Curia managed to circumvent the pope's own birth control commission. The Curia only proved once again that its historic skill in Vatican infighting gives it a tremendous advantage in protecting its own power and privilege. However, such skills no longer count for much. Apparently, Paul VI was persuaded that if he did not issue the encyclical, the credibility of Catholic sexual morality and indeed of the whole teaching authority of the papacy would be called into question. The advice was obviously completely mistaken, because few if any statements of the last half millennium have so badly injured the credibility of the papacy than the letter *Humanae Vitae*. The pathetic attempts of the papacy to obtain consent for the letter by appointing only bishops that supported it assumes that the clergy are prepared to take the bishops seriously as teachers of sexual morality. The data uncovered by our project suggest that they are no more willing to take the bishops seriously

on these matters than they are the pope. It will become increasingly hard to find potential bishops whose loyalty to *Humanae Vitae* is unquestioned, and if such loyalty continues to become the absolutely indispensable quality for promotion to the hierarchy, the quality of that august body will deteriorate still further.

Humanae Vitae is a misfortune not because priests and laity take it seriously. The image of the obedient Catholic laity bravely shouldering an almost impossible burden is simply invalid (no matter how much the pope and his advisers or his most extreme critics inside and outside the Church would have it so). *Humanae Vitae* was a tragedy rather because it destroyed for many Catholics and for many priests their confidence in ecclesiastical leadership, and brought to a definitive end the optimism and euphoria which Vatican Council II had engendered. *Humanae Vitae* is a symbol of the whole Pauline papacy: With all possible good intentions, Paul VI tried to slow down the pace of change so that the transition from the old to the new would be orderly, but he completely misread the strength and the direction of the forces the Council unleashed in the Church. Instead of creating orderly change, Paul VI turned a highly fluid, dynamic, and complicated situation into chaos— and it will be a long time before the pieces will be put back together again.

3. It is likely to be a very long time before the Church recaptures any kind of credibility as a teacher of sexual morality. Indeed, it must be said in all honesty that as long as the shadow of the *Humanae Vitae* prohibition hangs over the Church, there is not the slightest likelihood of any progress toward the reestablishment of credibility. The Catholic family movements, Cana and CFM, for example, are in sad disarray. Based in part on a theory of large families, Cana and CFM were moving in the sixties in the direction of some kind of Christian personalism (though in many instances, a rather shallow variety). *Humanae Vitae* brought an end to all of that, not so much

because the members felt the need to throw away their contraceptives, but because of the smashing blow of the pope's refusal to even seriously consider the question. In a Church where the papal figure is not as important as he has been for the last several hundred years, theoreticians would not have been so staggered by a papal encyclical. But in the Church of the 1960s, the papal authority figure still looms in gigantic proportion. The obstacles to the development of new theories are not legal but psychological. When the official Church appears to have closed its mind on the possibility of development of sexual teaching and remains rigidly fixated in the eighteenth century, the reaction of most theoreticians is to throw up their hands in despair and say, in effect, "Why bother to try?"

The result may very well be a period of pure permissiveness in which for want of anything better to say, priests will tell lay people that the Church is incapable of providing any kind of guidance in the sexual field, and that it is pretty much all right to do whatever they want. Our data do not show that such a phenomenon has occurred as yet; most priests still reject premarital sex, although young priests are somewhat more likely to approve of it than older priests.

But the important point is that there is no great demand for legitimation of premarital sex. Despite all the articles in the popular press to the contrary, there is no evidence that chastity is any less prevalent now than it was in the past—which is not to say that it ever has been all that prevalent. The overwhelming majority of Americans still believe, in theory if not in practice, in premarital chastity—probably as much as they did in the past and probably as much as they are going to in the future. Despite the widely publicized cohabitation among college students (one would think that they are the first group of young human beings in history to take lovers), the social norm against extramarital sex still stands, and hence the Catholic position is supported by the wider social position—a situation which is exactly opposite from the birth control question. In other words, at the present time the Roman Catholic Church has nothing persuasive or effective to add to general social norms of sexual morality. In the midst of Western man's frantic efforts to assimilate the wisdom of depth psychology and philosophical personalism, the only contribution the Catholic Church apparently is capable of making seems limited to a handwringing concern about the physical mechanics of procreation. Surely we could do better.

4. What is needed is a whole new theory of sexual morality, probably one less concerned with specific negative prohibitions and more concerned with the fascinating religious symbolism of human love as an image of the relationship between Christ and his Church and vice versa. Surely a Church which has an intercourse symbol of the lighted candle being plunged into water at the center of the Easter liturgy must have some wisdom to contribute to the human quest for a deeper understanding of the great mysteries of sexuality and love. It would not be fair to say that there is nothing being done by the psychologists, theologians, philosophers, and theoreticians toward developing a Christian vision of sexuality, but it would not be an exaggeration to say that very little is being done, and that little is likely to be done as long as the Church is bogged down in the swamps of *Humanae Vitae.* Most Catholics will continue to live lives of relative chastity under the influence of the general sexual norms of the society. Young Catholics will go through the sexual maturation process with no more wisdom available to them than is available to any of their fellow Americans. Bizarre aberrations, such as the nude marathon encounter, will have as much if not more appeal to the sexually confused Catholics as to their sexually confused fellow Americans. (One hears that at Esalon nuns are among the most enthusiastic frequenters of the nude marathon.) And the clergy, entrusted *ex officio* with the solemn responsibility of interpreting the

implications of the message of Jesus for human life, will have to shrug their shoulders and say that as far as they know, there are no special implications of the Good News for human sexuality. Bishops, aware that many of their priests will no longer attempt to impose the official position (though probably refusing to believe how extensive that refusal is), will awkwardly look the other way, knowing that the position went out of fashion long ago and that they have no real power to impose the papal decision on their priests.

RECOMMENDATIONS

1. At this point the encyclical *Humanae Vitae* is a dead letter, and there is no point in attempting to revoke it. What is needed rather is the beginning of a new approach in which the Holy See urges Catholic scholars and practitioners to begin to re-examine the Christian tradition and reformulate the sexual wisdom of that tradition in terms that provide assistance to modern man. It should encourage attempts to determine which methods of family planning are acceptable and which are unacceptable. This will almost certainly exceed the competence of Church authority. The Church must ask itself, given the present situation in which the traditional teaching as embodied by *Humanae Vitae* enjoys no credibility at all, where ought we to begin anew in our attempts to provide meaning and interpretation for human sexuality? Such new attempts obviously imply a de facto acceptance of the reality of the failure of *Humanae Vitae*, but recognizing that truth is far less important, it seems to me, than trying to begin again somewhere else.

2. It is probably essential to acknowledge that mistakes have been made. Indeed, I see no way for the Church to begin to re-establish credibility in the sexual area without acknowledging the horrendous mistakes of the past. I am not a theologian, and I do not propose to try to explain how such mistakes can be

harmonized with the Church's claim to infallibility, though heaven knows vast numbers of other mistakes have been made in the past. The fundamental concern, of course, for the sanctity of human life is not a mistake, but that concern has manifested itself in ways that clearly have been mistaken. A view of ecclesiastical authority which refuses to admit the possibility of mistakes in formulation is precisely that view which has got us into the present mess; it must be abandoned before we can extricate ourselves from it. Obviously, one can expect no progress during the present papacy.

3. The position of most priests is an extremely awkward one. They can, of course, give private advice in the confessional or in counseling sessions that are at variance with the official and public teaching of the Church. But they must be wary of how open they are with such advice. A peculiar, implicit gentleman's agreement has developed between clergy and hierarchy in which the hierarchy commits itself not to try to seriously enforce compliance with *Humanae Vitae* so long as the clergy is not too open and public in its opposition to the encyclical. Such an agreement may be necessary in the present organizational context of the Church, but it is a sad judgment on that organizational context that such devious, not to say dishonest, procedures have to be followed. I can think of no practical recommendation that can be made on the subject. Obviously, the long-range solution is to change the organizational context so that those whose cooperation is necessary for the implementation of any ecclesiastical decision will be deeply involved in making the decision—a principle of the human relations approach to organization which ought to be obvious even without the theology of collegiality.

But the ordinary priest can do little without leadership, scholarship, theory, or even the promise of a beginning of theory. Men and women being what they are, they will almost certainly continue to turn to their religious leaders for advice on their sexual problems, and the Catholic clergy are in a singularly bad position to give such advice. Their only consolation is that the human race has an excellent record for not taking seriously the advice of its religious leaders on a wide variety of subjects, most especially sexuality.

5

THE CELIBACY ISSUE

FINDINGS

1. Thirty-seven per cent of the diocesan priests (32 per cent of the religious) agree strongly that "celibacy should be a matter of personal choice for diocesan priests. Nineteen per cent of the diocesan priests (21 per cent of the religious) agree somewhat to the statement. Seven per cent of the diocesan and 9 per cent of the religious are uncertain. Ten per cent of the diocesan and 10 per cent of the religious disagree somewhat, and 28 per cent diocesan (and 28 per cent of the religious) disagree strongly with such an assertion. On the other hand, only 11 per cent of the bishops fall in the agree categories and 85 per cent fall in the disagree categories. Furthermore, there is a sharp age differential, with three fifths of the priests under thirty-five strongly in favor of change and three fifths of the priests over fifty-five strongly opposed.

2. About two thirds of the priests in the country expect a change in the laws of celibacy, and three quarters of those expect it to take place within the next ten years. On the other hand, only 18 per cent of the bishops expect a change. Eighty-eight per cent of the priests under thirty-five and 76 per cent of those between thirty-six and forty-five expect a change.

3. Twenty-two per cent of the priests (and one third of those

between twenty-six and thirty-five) say they would marry if they were free to do so.

4. The majority of priests agree that celibacy is an advantage for doing their work better, for personal growth and development, for development of their love of God, and for relating more fully to other people. Overwhelming support (78 per cent of all priests, 73 per cent of those between twenty-six and thirty-five) exists for only the first of the reasons listed—"for doing my work better."

5. The majority of priests favor an option for those who have resigned the priesthood to marry that would permit these men to return.

6. The majority also think that the present requirement of celibacy keeps many men from entering the priesthood who would actually make excellent priests, and that celibacy may in fact be harmful to some priests.

7. Only a tiny percentage of priests (4 or 5 per cent) are involved in dating or courtship relationships.

8. In summary, priests tend to support and expect change in the celibacy regulation, but only a minority of them see this as a matter that has importance for their own personal lives. Celibacy is still valued in the clergy; the overwhelming majority, even among the younger ones, see it as an advantage to them in their work. Apparently many of those who support a change do so because they are not convinced that celibacy is essential to the priesthood, and because they think celibacy can be harmful for some priests and is keeping many men out of the priesthood. In other words, the change in the celibacy regulation is perceived as being desirable for the Church if not necessarily desirable for oneself.

SPECULATIONS

1. Perhaps it is appropriate for me to begin by saying that if I were filling out the NORC questionnaire, my response would

have been "agree somewhat" with the statement "celibacy should be a matter of personal choice for the diocesan priest." My agreement is qualified with the adverb "somewhat" not so much because I do not believe that celibacy ought to be optional as because I believe the issue is an exceedingly comlicated one and that not enough attention has been paid to the complexities of it in the present debate. Indeed, the celibacy issue has been made a political symbol in the present conflict between the old and the new in the Church. Unfortunately, one rarely if ever hears much rational discussion of the complexities of political symbols; however, ecclesiastical authority has only itself to blame for the politicization of the celibacy issue. Its adamant refusal to engage in responsible, open discussion of the subject is primarily to blame for the practical impossibility of finding an intelligent solution to the controversy.

Celibacy is yet another example of what happened to an absolute obligation imposed without the need for justification or explanation by pure authority. While I am inclined to agree with those who think that the Church can legitimately make the charisma of celibacy a condition for ordination, I also think that such an obligation cannot be expected to obtain consent in a dynamic and open Church unless the theoretical justification is much more elaborate than that presently available to us. Once again, the theorists became sloppy. It was enough that priests were celibate without having to try to constantly rethink the psychological, sociological, philosophical, and theological justifications for celibacy. When the ability of authority to impose its regulations without question collapsed in the wake of the Vatican Council (and the Americanization of the immigrant groups), there simply was no theory available to make a persuasive case for celibacy. And Paul VI responded characteristically by attempting to reassert an absolute authority he no longer possessed, thereby making a bad situation even worse.

For

More Freedom

To say that there is persuasive theoretical justification for celibacy at the present time is not to argue that there is no wisdom in either the tradition of the Church or in the personal experience of many priests that support celibacy. On the contrary, both the personal experience of many of us and the data gathered in our survey would indicate that there is powerful if frequently inarticulate support for celibacy as a good thing for the Church. Indeed, many of those who are in favor of change want it more because it would increase the amount of free options available rather than because they themselves are planning to exercise those options. In other words, the celibacy issue has become a symbol of personal freedom—and the ecclesiastical authorities have only themselves to thank for this development.

The data in our study show that most priests are able to maintain a distinction between optional celibacy and compulsory marriage. They do not want to see the end of celibacy in the Church; they simply want to see its end as an obligation. Unfortunately, much of the discussion on the subject, particularly the contribution made by some liberal laity, obscures this distinction, for it seems that many of the most vigorous public proponents of optional celibacy are really seeking a situation where there is not so much the possibility of a married clergy but where virtually all clergy would be married. This is clearly not what the majority of our respondents have in mind.

2. But it may be actually what will happen if celibacy is made optional, and this is the principal reason why I would "agree somewhat." The experience of many of the other churches, including the Anglican and the Greek Orthodox, is not only that most priests marry eventually (in the Orthodox Church, before their ordination), it is that most priests who want to work in parishes have no choice but to marry. Charles Merrill Smith in his somewhat cynical but shrewd book, *How to Become a Bishop Without Being Religious*, summarized the

reasons why there is little real option for celibacy once a married clergy becomes possible:

If by now you are contemplating the advantages of clerical celibacy (which would not be an unreasonable reaction considering the problems involved in your selection) dismiss such thoughts at once. Protestant Christians expect their clergy to marry. The folklore of the trade holds that it is necessary for a minister to marry in order to set an example of Christian family life.

You will want to pretend that this is true, just as you will find it expedient to pretend that you dwell in a state of marital bliss, the calm waters of which are never rippled by a cross word, let alone a quarrel. The nervous strain involved in such pretensions is of awesome proportions, and is known to have pushed parsonage wives into emotional breakdowns and turned parsonage children into church-hating delinquents. However, all good things in this life are bought at a price.

The real reasons why you should marry are, of course, not at all related to the folklore.

First, a clergyman who remains unmarried for more than a year after graduation from seminary is suspected of being abnormal, immoral or chicken.

Second, there will be those who will speculate that he has taken St. Paul on marriage too seriously and has made a secret vow of celibacy. So far as your parishioners are concerned, you may be as celibate as a Cistercian monk, but they will insist that you practice it within the married state.

Third, somewhat more than half of your congregation will be women, and all women—single, married or widowed (including grass widows)—resent a male eligible for marriage who chooses to remain unwed.

Fourth—and here is the overriding argument in the mind of the congregation—since the church owns a parsonage and already has arrived at a salary figure below which it cannot go and maintain its conviction, however illusory, that it is a humane institution, it is only sensible to get two employees for the price of one. Therefore, it boils down to a business proposition. It would be damaging and vulgar to admit to this, however, so the tradition and the folklore were manufactured to mask it.

Actually it is very good business from the church's point of view. Most girls are piano players of sorts, and anyone can learn to operate a typewriter or mimeograph. Add to these accomplishments the intellectually untaxing duties of Sunday school teaching, choir singing, ladies' aid work and a miscellany of other small parish chores, all of which your wife will be expected in your first small churches to perform (it's part of the tradition) and you have a job analysis which, were it filled by a salaried employee, would require no small addition to the annual budget. Hence the tradition of a married clergy. . . . If you want to be a preacher and a bachelor, be prepared for a dismal future and renounce now the hope for status, prestige, emolument, luxury and all of the spiritual joys which accompany a plush suburban pastorate. The author does not question the preacher's right to take a vow of chastity, but he'd better darn well understand that a vow of poverty goes along with it.[1]

I doubt that many Protestant ministers would seriously question what Smith says, though they may not appreciate the humorous tone. It seems to me that precious little attention is paid to this problem in present political advocacy for a change in clerical celibacy. Whenever the issue is raised—and that is rarely—the easy reply is offered: The Catholic tradition is different than that of either the Orthodox or Protestant traditions, and one can expect both married and unmarried will exist in the Catholic Church for an indefinite future. But I am not so sure this is possible, and while I do believe that in the contemporary world there should be a minimum of obligation and a maximum of option, I think it will be an immense task, for which the Church is now singularly unprepared, to keep alive a tradition of a partially celibate parish clergy once celibacy becomes an option. Most priests who advocate a change in the celibacy law are still in favor of a continuation of celibacy as a viable option even for parish priests, but they do not seem to be aware of the immense difficulties that will stand in the way of such a continuance; and few seem ready to face the strong likelihood that optional celibacy may very

[1] Charles Merrill Smith, *How to Become a Bishop Without Being Religious* (Garden City, N.Y., Doubleday & Company, Inc., 1965), pp. 21–23.

well mean obligatory marriage for the parish clergy, if not in the short run then surely in the long run.

3. Nor does there seem to be much awareness of the experience of our Protestant brothers with the stress and strain that a minister's wife and family must endure. There is an extensive literature on the subject (including, for example, the doctoral dissertation of Professor Ross Scherer on the Lutheran Church-Missouri Synod clergy.) In addition to the extreme difficulty of raising children on the very limited salaries that the Protestant clergy receive and the need to constantly be on the lookout for promotion, if only so that one could somehow afford to send one's children to college, the minister has little choice but to accept the fact that his wife and children are religious functionaries even if they don't want to be. Again, Smith's somewhat cynical comments merely reflect a great deal of what can be read in the empirical literature:

> If you find yourself in the difficult position of beginning your ministry equipped with a wife you married because you fancied you were in love, or because you found her charming, or because you were sexually attracted to her, or for any other irrelevant reason, you are up against what will probably turn out to be the most baffling problem of your professional life. Barring the unlikely possibility that by chance and blind luck you picked the right type for the parsonage (which would be the equivalent of breaking the bank at Monte Carlo or filling an inside straight) about all you can do now is to institute a program of education designed to bring her up to minimum standards of performance . . .
>
> However, you should be cautioned against excessive optimism as to the probable results. Observation of such educational efforts have been depressing; the woman who marries a minister without understanding the nature of the demands his profession places on her usually proving quite intractable when it is suggested, even with considerable tact, that she make over her personality to the satisfaction of her husband's present and anticipated congregations.[2]

[2] Ibid., pp. 19–20.

I do not raise these problems as an argument against optional celibacy, but more as a clarification of my somewhat ambivalent support for it. I would at least wish that in the present discussion there was more concern paid to both the economic and organizational question as well as to the very grave strains and tensions imposed on a clergyman's wife and family. However, most of the discussion goes on with the romantic assumption that where true love is concerned, no obstacles will ever stand in the way.

I reject the argument of some ecclesiastics that the real reason for maintaining obligatory celibacy is financial. The idea that the Catholic clergy are cheap labor slaves who cannot marry because the Church will not pay them more I find repulsive. There should be some awareness, however, that if the clergy are permitted to marry, they will live under strain of anything from extreme to serious financial privation. Also, to be a clergyman's wife is at least as much a religious vocation as to be a clergyman.

4. Nor can I accept the argument that a married clergyman is as free to serve his people as a celibate clergyman. Such an argument, I think, can be made only by those who do not have families of their own and who have never paid much attention to what the obligations of family life entail. The married clergyman may be as dedicated as a celibate, but he simply does not have as much time, nor, for that matter, as much freedom of movement. Anyone who says he does is ignorant of the obligations of family life. (Catholic radicals like the Berrigan brothers have repeatedly insisted on the importance of celibacy in their lives as providing them with freedom for action that a man with family responsibilities would hesitate to take. While I do not happen to agree with the particular action the Berrigan brothers have chosen, I think a similar assertion could be made by many other priests.)

Finally, the argument that a dedicated doctor or lawyer can be intensely committed to his clients and at the same time be a responsible family man is a very dubious sort of argument.

One may, of course, successfully blend the roles of professional man and family man, but I think one can do so only by drawing severe limits on one's professional commitments.

5. Nor do I think a decision on the celibacy problem can be made without wide consultation among the laity. It has always seemed to me that most of those clergymen who are so vigorously supporting a change in the celibacy rule are also committed, in theory at least, to wider lay participation in the Church, but they show precious little inclination to deal the laity into the discussion of the possibility of optional celibacy. I am inclined to suspect—on the basis of a single question asked in a Harris study in 1967—that a bare majority of the laity could live with the idea of a married clergy. It would seem to me that this rather thin margin of support for such a change (and the margin may have grown wider in recent years) would only constitute the barest sort of beginning of lay participation in the discussion of the complexities and the implications of optional celibacy. Of course, if one believes that a priest has the absolute right to get married, a right which overrides both his own commitment and the Church's power to establish conditions for ordination, then obviously what the lay people think doesn't make a damn bit of difference. However, those of us who would support optional celibacy, not so much because we think marriage is an absolute right as because we think that options are more human than obligations, have no choice but to include the laity as having every right for being concerned about what happens. As in so many other aspects of our study, it would have been of immense help if data on lay attitudes and values had been available to us.

6. Finally, I am not sure that such a change of major importance can be imposed on the Church by a simple majority, with only a little more than 50 per cent of the clergy supporting a change and only a minority strongly supporting such a change. Major changes in any human institution require broad consensus rather than simple majorities, and at the present time a

broad consensus does not exist, although it may within the next decade. However, consensus will emerge more quickly if the celibacy issue could be taken out of the area of political militancy and returned to where it belongs, the area of rational discussion. I am not hopeful about this occurring. The opportunity to make the celibacy issue a rational discussion was probably lost in 1967 when the pope issued his encyclical asserting that the celibacy issue was closed. He did not realize then and may not yet realize that whatever may have been said of the past, it is no longer possible for a pope to prevent discussion.

RECOMMENDATIONS

1. Celibacy ought to become an open question. By this I mean that the papacy and the hierarchy ought to be willing to concede that there are some distinctive advantages in making celibacy an option, and even some distinct advantages in having married priests. On the other hand, those who are most vigorously advocating optional celibacy for the day after tomorrow should face the fact that there are many and serious problems in such a change. If one could get admissions like these from both sides of the controversy, then rational discussion might return and scholarly investigation might once again become possible, though heaven knows that in the absence of any well-thought-out theory of sexuality, one can scarcely expect a well-thought-out theory of celibacy. Unless I am mistaken, there is not much chance for the celibacy issue to become an open question in the sense that I mean. Certainly nothing that happened at the meeting of the bishops in Detroit in the spring of 1971 gave any indication that they were willing to engage in serious and open dialogue on the subject. This chapter is being written before the Episcopal Synod in Rome, and I see no sign that Rome will be any different than Detroit. While there are excesses on both sides in the present celibacy controversy, it must be emphasized that the refusal of the leadership to discuss the

question has made it impossible for most priests who would probably take a moderate position to do anything but support the most vehement and simple demands for change. In other words, it will take an initiative from the leadership to make celibacy an open question once again. No one should hold his breath waiting for it.

2. While discussion continues (in the naïve assumption that it will begin), there ought to be experimentation, not just with the ordination of married men but also with the provision that priests in certain kinds of work might marry, or that some priests who wish to marry might be assigned to some special service. It might, for example, be decided that when a priest wishes to marry, a diocesan board would determine whether he would be permitted to leave the priesthood with honor in order to marry or be invited to continue in the priesthood in some special kind of work. One way, of course, to preserve celibacy in parochial clergy would be to use the opposite system the Greeks use, that is to permit marriage for those not in the parochial ministry and requiring celibacy of those who volunteer for parish work. I should emphasize that these are only very tentative suggestions for discussion, and scarcely detailed blueprints for action.

3. I should also like to see more consideration to the possibility of limited service ministry. Ours is a culture of short-range decisions. A man rarely makes a lifelong commitment to a job, to a company, to a house, to a city, or even an area of the country any more. The only lifelong commitment he makes is to his spouse, and such shrewd observers as Warren Bennis (provost of State University of New York at Buffalo) ask whether in a "temporary society" even that sort of long-range commitment can be expected to continue. (I think Bennis is wrong on this point, and I am not so sure that society is quite so temporary as he seems to feel.) While marriage may be an exception to the short-range decisions, it is so only because of

the unique relationship between two persons involved in a marriage commitment.

In a society of such short-term commitments, it may be unreasonable to expect young people in their early twenties to make a presumably permanent and irrevocable commitment either to the priesthood or the religious life—and it may be equally unreasonable to expect the Church to make a permanent long-range commitment to them. Why would it not be possible for young men and women to equip themselves for service to the Church for five years, with an option on both sides to renew the contract—perhaps after ten years, the Church would offer "tenure" by which it would offer support for as long as the person cared to remain a religious functionary. There is of course no problem at all with limited term service to the religious life, though there is, I am told by theologians, a problem with limited term service to the priesthood: A man, it is said, becomes a priest permanently. But even under such circumstances, it does not seem to me that a man necessarily commits himself permanently to the exercise of the ministry. May he not be given an option of exercising it on a renewable basis?

For all practical purposes we have such a situation now. Both legally and socially it is very easy to leave the priesthood if one wants to. Might it not be wise to recognize the reality of such ease of exit and make it a matter of policy? I have a hunch that short-term commitment to the priesthood and the religious life would attract many more young people than are presently inclined to a religious or priestly vocation. Very considerable numbers of them would renew their contracts. Obviously, experimentation along these lines (and all I suggest is experimentation) could exist under circumstances either of obligatory or of optional celibacy. I would most like to see a continuation of the celibacy obligation for the parochial clergy, together with the option of short-term service; but let me emphasize that such a scheme is a highly speculative point for discussion. It is not a policy for immediate implementation.

Unfortunately, the present political situation is not conducive for discussion or speculation. What we have rather is unnegotiable demands on one side and a refusal to discuss on the other. Furthermore, it does not seem likely that the situation will change. Celibacy may be lost in the Western Church to be rediscovered again many centuries hence. If such is the event, it will be a great misfortune, and we will only have ourselves to blame.

6

ATTITUDES: RELIGIOUS, SOCIAL, AND ECUMENICAL

FINDINGS

1. We could find little loss of "faith" among priests; that is to say, most of them were still willing to endorse statements which resembled orthodox doctrinal formulations.

2. However, many priests, especially the younger ones, are far more likely to agree with values that emphasize process rather than substance, existence rather than essence, open-endedness rather than immutability. At the bishops' meeting in Detroit, one hierarch remarked that a theologian was "an existentialist," as though that virtually made him a heretic. In fact, however, as a rough estimate, one might say that about half of our respondents accept an emphasis that is essentially existential.

3. Bishops, however, are much less likely to take an existentialist stand. Sixty-nine per cent of the bishops and only 45 per cent of the priests agreed that "faith means essentially belief in the doctrines of the Catholic Church," whereas 46 per cent of the bishops and 69 per cent of the priests would agree that faith is "primarily an encounter with God and Christ Jesus rather than an assent to a coherent set of defined truths."

4. There is moderately strong support for and involvement

in ecumenism among the clergy, with both stronger support and more involvement to be found among the hierarchy. This is perhaps because the position and responsibilities of bishops bring them into more frequent contact with their Protestant counterparts.

5. On two questions measuring attitudes toward a guaranteed annual wage and racial disturbances in the cities, bishops took a "more progressive" stand than the priests, while they in their turn were more progressive than a sample of lay people.

6. There is a strong relationship, as one might expect, between age and a score on a "modern" values index.[1] Age explains a massive 40 per cent of the variants on this index, but it follows that there is a generation slope rather than gap between older and younger clergy, with each successively younger age cohort being more "modern" than its predecessor. If one compares those under thirty with those over fifty-five, there is a gap, but if one looks at each five-year age cohort (as one should do), one sees there is no dichotomy between old and young, but rather a gradual change through time.

7. There is an obvious generation gap, however, between the younger clergy and the bishops. It is not a gap that can be explained simply in terms of their different ages. On most attitudes toward religion and sexual morality, bishops are more "conservative" than men of their own age groups.

8. Curiously enough, on attitudes toward ecumenism and the guaranteed annual wage, bishops are more "liberal" than priests under thirty-five.

SPECULATIONS

1. Almost 70 per cent of the priests were willing to accept in theory the assertion that faith is an orientation of the total personality rather than assent to certain basic truths. Neverthe-

[1] An index which measures basically an essentialist versus existentialist response pattern.

less, however justified such a position may be even in pre-Conciliar theology, it still remains true that most of our training in schools and in seminaries emphasized acceptance of doctrinal propositions as a measure of faith. Indeed, whole, elaborate systems indicating the various levels of ascent to different kinds of truths were developed. As I remember, the lowest level of truth was the proposition that was *comunissima* and *certissima*, which meant "most common" and "most certain." For some peculiar reason, something that was *communissima* and *certissima* was less certain than something *communis* and *certa*, "common" and "certain." There is a Wonderland quality about a world in which something that is most certain is less certain than something that is certain. (There were other elements of Wonderland in the pre-Vatican Church too, some more important than "theological notes.")

By the criteria of accepting doctrines, most priests still have the "faith." By the criteria of the orientation of the total personality and God is manifested in the message of Jesus, the matter is more obscure. Instruments do not exist to measure such existential commitment, and if the truth be told, such commitment was not all that important in the post-Tridentine immigrant Church. The social structure and the culture of Catholicism were such that the bare minimum of personal commitment was all that was required. The external constraints and supports guaranteed appropriate behavior in the absence of powerful internal motivations. Faith may very well be a problem for many of us, not in the sense that we reject explicit doctrinal formulations but in the sense that we find it very hard to shift in the middle years of life from an externally supported faith to an internally committed faith. Survey research is not yet advanced enough in its methodology to be able to deal with such a complex question; however, if I understand what Father Kennedy and the Loyola psychology department team has told us, their findings substantiate the notion of how important this shift from external to internal control is in the present crisis in the priesthood.

I am not suggesting that those who leave the priesthood are doing so because they have "problems of faith." As we shall see, 40 per cent of the resigned priests still attend church every week, 40 per cent more still consider themselves to be in some way or another Christian. It may very well be that resignation from the priesthood for some men may in fact represent a maturation of their religious faith. Similarly, staying in the priesthood may for some men be a refusal to mature religiously, while for others it may be the logical result of religious maturation.

To put the matter more bluntly, the changes both in American society at the end of the immigrant era and in the Church Universal with the end of the Counter Reformation have forced many of us to face more openly than we ever expected to have to do the question of whether we really do accept the graciousness of being as proclaimed in the person and message of Jesus. This, of course, *is* the fundamental question, and how we respond to that question may be quite independent of how we react to certain doctrinal formulations. There is not much evidence in our research that doctrinal formulations are a problem for many priests. In that respect, faith (here understood in the very narrow sense of the term) is not part of the present crisis; but in the sense of re-examining the message of Jesus and our acceptance of the graciousness of being, it is my impression that faith is a problem for many of us, an impression backed up by the Loyola research. If it is a problem, it can turn out to be one of growth and not of decline of religious commitment.

2. That there is a very strong correlation between age and the modern value scale ought not to be very surprising. The existentialist process-oriented vocabulary used in the items measuring the "modern" end of the scale would be a vocabulary that young priests would be much more likely to be at ease with

than older priests. A priest my age (forty-three) and older would understand the vocabulary of the new theological emphasis only if he had made a vigorous effort to keep up with his reading. But whether the difference in vocabulary measures anything more than one's familiarity with the current theological jargon, perhaps even the currently fashionable clichés, is another and more difficult question to answer. A man may be very existential in his life and still feel much more at ease with traditional religious formulations, while a younger man may be rather narrow in his personality structure but quite up to date in his vocabulary. To some extent it is even possible that the differences between old and young on the personality scale discussed in a previous chapter are in fact differences in familiarity with approved responses rather than any fundamental personality difference. There is no simple method in determining whether a response pattern measures different fundamental values and orientations or merely different levels of vocabulary sophistication. Any sophisticated researcher working with scales put together from opinion items has sense enough to be very cautious in his interpretations of differences on these scales. All I would be prepared to say on the basis of our data is that there is a tendency for the younger clergy to use a rather different set of categories to formulate their religious convictions, and that these differences in vocabulary *may* represent profoundly different orientations about God, Church, and priesthood. Furthermore, while my own sympathies are more likely to be with the existentialist perspective rather than the essentialist one, I would not want to claim any inherent superiority for my own perspective. I would be content with asserting that it seems somewhat more useful to the needs of our own times, particularly as manifested by the younger generation of lay people. What is important about a religious symbol is not so much its express content as what a man does with it. A supposedly existentialist open-ended formulation can be used just as easily to club others into submission as can phrases taken right out of the Baltimore Catechism. On the other hand, the phrases of the Baltimore Catechism were a step to authentic and fully human religiousness for many people in the past and for some today. All things being equal, I am inclined to think that the newer formulations provide deeper insight into the basic Christian symbols, but when one is dealing with real human beings, all other things are never equal.

No one who has lived in a rectory or attended clerical gatherings can be under any illusion about how much conflict rages around these different religious formulations. In most instances the two groups which seem to emerge most often in such clerical bull sessions are talking past one another. Rarely if ever is there any attempt made to understand the other man's position from within his own perspective. Of course, the clergy have no monopoly on the substitution of argumentation for communication, and there are differences among age groups of the clergy which are not merely verbal. Nonetheless, those differences might not be so great if those who felt more at ease with traditional formulations were patient enough to try to grasp the inner logic of the more existential formulations. They may discover that those formulations, no matter how shocking they may seem, can often admit of authentically Christian interpretation. On the other hand, it might also be helpful if those of us who are so enthused about a process-oriented religious vocabulary could occasionally attempt a translation into categories that their senior colleagues might more easily understand. They may discover that while the new symbol system may be useful for their own generation, it does not follow that it is the only symbol system that has any use or that no purpose was ever served by alternative symbol systems. To put it bluntly, more people should shut up and listen.

3. I have considerable reservations therefore about some of the uses made of attitudinal and value scales in research on the clergy and the religious. The high correlations found among

some of these scales seem to have struck some researchers as a major and important social discovery. That those with "pre-Vatican" tendencies on an attitudinal scale are less likely to endorse certain social and political positions may be nothing more than that they are less familiar with the approved vocabularies in both religious and social matters. I do not say that such a cautious and conservative interpretation is the only one possible, but I think it is important for social researchers to acknowledge the crudity of their tools and be cautious with the interpretations they draw in the use of such tools. One writer, for example, after having read a summary of *American Priests* concluded from the fact that those who are inclined to resign from the priesthood have a higher score on the "modern" religious value scales and that therefore the "best" priests are resigning. Such an interpretation may not be completely out of the question, but I think it is one that no responsible researcher would dare to make. Indeed, the only appropriate conclusion, it seems to me, would be that those who tend to use contemporary religious formulations are also more likely to resign from the priesthood. Unfortunately, such sophistication about the interpretation of sociological data does not seem to be widespread in the population, and on occasion deems to be singularly lacking among certain kinds of researchers.[2]

4. The pattern of clergy being more liberal on racial and social matters than the laity is widespread among American religious denominations. Jeffrey Hadden, for example, has documented this phenomenon among Protestant ministers in his *The Gathering Storm in the Churches*. It may come as a surprise to some readers, however, to discover that the pattern persists among Catholics. And even more astonishing is that the hierarchy are even more "progressive" on the two racial

---

[2] Incidentally, the correlation between modern values and resignation declines from .47 to .26 when age is held constant, suggesting that to some considerable extent "modernism" is merely a variable that intervenes between age and resignation.

and welfare items on our questionnaire than the clergy. There are a number of different possible explanations. It may be that from their positions as heads of dioceses they see more clearly the nature and impact of social problems than do many priests at the grass roots who are not in direct contact with those problems. It may also be that the bishops find it somewhat easier to take a progressive stand than does the parish priest who is in direct contact with the more conservative social instincts of many of his parishioners. It may also be that the hierarchy are more conscious of the social action tradition of the American Church, represented by such historic giants as John Ireland, Lancaster Spaulding, and John Ryan. However, the phenomenon of the bishop who tends to be quite progressive on social action matters and very conservative on religious and sexual matters is widespread enough in the American hierarchy to make our findings plausible. Even though the famous 1918 and 1939 statements of the American hierarchy on social problems may not represent the social views of all bishops then or now, they nonetheless provide justification for a tradition of social concern. There is no such traditional justification for a shift in sexual ethics or doctrinal formulations—at least not yet.

5. More difficult to understand is the greater commitment of bishops to ecumenism. Perhaps the best explanation is a structural one: Given the organization of American society, religious leaders of various denominations are under considerable pressure to participate in civic functions and work with members of other denominations. Social welfare committees, highway openings, inauguration of mayors, and even football games provide occasions for acquaintanceship and interaction which the normal parish priest or priest-teacher is not likely to encounter. It may simply be that there is more opportunity for ecumenical involvement and ecumenical concern on the diocesan level than there is on the grass roots level.

There has been very little research on the sociology of ecumenism. It will be important in the future to undertake such research if the ecumenical movement is not to run aground on the shoals of disappointment and discouragement, for unity among Christians (at least in the United States) will not be accomplished merely by dialogue among theologians or dinner parties among bureaucrats. The social, cultural, and historical forces making for denominationalism are much stronger I suspect at the grass roots than they are among upper echelon bureaucrats and scholars. One may attend a meeting of Old Testament scholars and find it very difficult to distinguish Lutheran from Methodist; American Baptist from Catholic; yet one would still hear very different sermons from the New Testament in the individual churches of that group. The Lutheran Church-Missouri Synod, the Presbyterian, and the Catholic Church bureaucrat might have a delightful time in the bar after a national ecumenical conference. It would not be unlikely, however, to find not too far from the hotel churches of those respective denominations whose pastors barely know one another. Denominationalism is very much a part of the religio-ethnic structure of American society.[3] It is not likely to go away simply because doctrinal differences have been resolved or organizational schemes have been hedged. The long history of American denominationalism shows that most attempts at church mergers produce more rather than fewer denominations, because when two or more denominations come together, what often results is not one but three denominations. Intransient members of both denominations set up their own "pure, unadulterated" form of Christianity that they refuse to be let watered down by merger—and frequently what is pure and unadulterated would appear trivial to the outsider, but it has become an important symbol of cultural and social differences.

This has led me to suspect that the future of ecumenism in the United States is one of denominational ecumenism. There

[3] Andrew M. Greeley, *The Denominational Society* (Glenview, Ill., Scott, Foresman and Company, 1972).

may very well be some merging of mainline denominations of the sort anticipated by COCU (the Consultation on Church Unity), but there will be a long, long wait before such groups as the Southern Baptists, the Pentecostals, the Missouri Synod Lutherans, and the high-church Anglicans sit together around one banquet table for a liturgy to be presided over by the local Roman Catholic bishop.

The denominational approach to ecumenism may be a very constructive and creative one. I have always felt that the different denominations have different important contributions to make to American religious life. It would be a shame, for example, to lose the sort of tough, manly biblical Christianity that the male high school teachers in the Missouri Synod denominational schools so vigorously display. As a sociologist, I would like at least to inquire from the ecumenical theologians whether there could not be authentic religious unity while at the same time there would continue valid denominational diversity. Here, obviously, I am in direct disagreement with what is probably the mainstream of American ecumenical thinking, a mainstream which laments with the late H. Richard Niebuhr the proliferation of denominations. There is probably an outer limit of the number of desirable denominations, but on balance I am inclined to think that denominationalism is frequently more a sign of vitality than of perversity. Indeed, just as the genius of American political structure is to have found a way in which vastly diverse religious, racial, and ethnic groups can live in some sort of minimal harmony and tranquillity, it may well be that the ecclesiastical genius of the United States has been to produce a situation in which many religious denominations can live first of all at peace with each other and then make a constructive contribution to each other's growth through honest and respectful dialogue.

In my book *The Denominational Society* I argue that denominational pluralism antedated political and cultural pluralism and created a context in which these latter pluralisms could emerge.

It was precisely the religious diversity of the thirteen original states which (along with, of course, the economic and geographical diversity) forced those who framed our culture and our Constitution to create a pluralistic society. We have always been ambivalent about that pluralism, and while in theory we endorse the right of the ethnic immigrant groups to retain much of their own heritage, in practice we frequently pressure the ethnics to act like "us." I often find myself wondering whether that variety of ecumenism which wishes to eliminate denominational diversity is not a close cultural relative of the melting pot theory. It would seem to me to be much more appropriate to respect the religious and cultural diversity in our society, to realize that it is not likely to go away, and then to study it carefully to see if we may not learn from it.

I think an idea not unlike this just barely escaped condemnation in a papal encyclical some three quarters of a century ago. They called it "Americanism."

RECOMMENDATIONS

There is but one recommendation I have to make to conclude this chapter. Somewhere in the country, perhaps at one of the great Catholic universities, there ought to be built the best theological faculty in all the world, composed of scholars with the highest academic qualifications who will eschew political propaganda and the working out of their own psychological problems to address themselves to those questions especially pertinent for the American Catholic population.

I would like to see these theologians engage in their professional activity from the context of sympathetic understanding of the American Catholic experience. To do that they would probably need the opportunity to interact frequently with historians and sociologists who specialize in the study of American Catholicism—if they could find some. It is to be hoped that these theologians—scriptural scholars, systematic theologians, ascetical theologians, moral theologians—would either themselves be concerned about the reformulation of the Christian message in terms appropriate to the American environment, or at least they would work closely with the writers of popular spirituality and educational programs to see that materials presented to the masses of the Catholic population be both sound, tasteful, and relevant. (Which is, I think, the only time I shall use that much overworked word.)

When such a faculty comes into existence, one would hope that there might be some decline in the willingness of clergy to hurl frequently meaningless clichés at one another, and a decline in the willingness of many religious educators to tell Catholic masses what they no longer need to believe instead of telling them what the Christian message is. Shallow, superficial, unscholarly, phony theologizing is likely to be driven out only by the real thing. My years of experience as one of the editors of the international journal *Concilium* have persuaded me that however admirable the European theologians are and however useful to us their writings may be, the problems of cultural and structural translation are far more serious than the problems of literary translation. Therefore, a theology which will be pertinent to the American Church will have to be one that is developed by Americans on American soil, indeed, with interaction among European colleagues but not in slavish dependence on them.

One would have thought that with over three hundred institutions of higher education, 10 per cent of which claim to be major universities, we would have put together a faculty of that sort long ago. That we have not, are not in the process of doing so, and probably will not in the foreseeable future is both a measure of the futility of present behavior in the American Church and of its uncertain future in the American environment.

7

AUTHORITY, STRUCTURE, AND POWER
IN THE LIFE OF A PRIEST

FINDINGS

1. One of the most surprising findings in our research was that there was practically no appreciable relationship between loneliness, the desire to marry, propensity to resign, morale, and similar phenomena on the one hand and structural variables on the other. Such factors as region of the country, size of the diocese, proportion of religious priests in the diocese, the authority structure of the diocese, the number of associate pastors in the diocese, the length of time one had to wait to become a pastor, and many other similar structural items did not correlate at an important level with the dependent variables mentioned in the first sentence, and hence were dropped from our causal model. My colleague Richard Schoenherr, who is a specialist in the study of formal organizations, was less surprised than I because, as he tells me, the organizational literature has it that while size, for example, may affect the organizational structure of human institutions there is much less relationship between size and personal attributes of people who are members of the institution. In any event, despite widespread impressions to the contrary among priests, there is little relation between institutional structure and resignation from the priesthood or any similar attitudinal and behavioral variables. Furthermore, per-

haps even more surprising, is that there seemed to be no relationship between the dependent variables we were especially concerned with and the amount of postordination education or the kind of work one did. Popular mythology, of course, says that those with advanced degrees are the ones most likely to contemplate resignation, and that associate pastors are more likely to think of leaving the priesthood than pastors. In fact, neither variable correlated with resignation anywhere in our causal model.[1] That size, organizational structure, education, and "occupation" do not correlate consistently with our dependent variables may be the most important negative finding of the study.[2] The reader can be quite confident that we double and triple checked to make sure the finding was valid.

2. If structure, authority, and the distribution of power do not have an appreciable impact on propensity to resign, it does not follow that they are not important dimensions of the life of the Church; it merely follows that they are not predictors of resignation.

3. There is no evidence that priests wish to do away with authority in the Church.

4. There is considerable evidence, however, indeed overwhelming evidence, that priests want to see a much wider distribution of the use of authority in the Church.

5. The priests' senate seems to be an especially important concern of priests in their desire for wider distribution of power and authority in the Church.

[1] Those who have already resigned from the priesthood tended to have somewhat more advanced education than those who remained in it. The fact that there is no correlation between education and plans to leave for those who are presently priests suggests that in the early stages of the upsurge of resignations, advanced degree training has impact—perhaps because those with advanced degrees were more confident of the marketability of their skills—but that as the resignations have continued, these factors are no longer a pertinent aspect of inclination to resign.

[2] As we shall note later on, on two measures—morale and work satisfaction—there is a correlation with being an associate pastor. However, associate pastor does not correlate with loneliness, desire to marry, or propensity to resign from the priesthood.

6. Bishops, on the other hand, are willing to admit theoretically that there is a need for greater decentralization of power, but they do not seem to be inclined to support many specific changes in the power structure. They are by and large inclined to think that the present practical distribution of power is ideal. They are not, in other words, greatly dissatisfied with the way decisions are made in the Church.

7. Therefore, since there is disagreement between the leadership and followers on both the practical distribution of power and the helpfulness of structural reform, and since there is a heavy concentration of power in the hands of leadership, and since there is a widespread tendency to ignore unpopular resignations, and, finally, since there is widespread and generalized disagreement between priests and bishops on many religious and ethical issues, one must conclude that there is indeed a situation of polarization between clergy and hierarchy, one that might even be considered dangerous.

8. Eighty-six per cent of the priests in our sample advocated the introduction of a married diaconate, 78 per cent supported a court of appeals distinct from the hierarchy guaranteeing due processes of law, and 70 per cent advocated some married priests working on a variety of ministries, election of pope by the Synod of Bishops, and election of bishops by priests of the diocese. Sixty-five per cent advocated that the religious and laity also participate in such elections, and 64 per cent supported the so-called "household ministries," or small group parishes. On the other hand, only about one fifth advocated the elimination of Catholic schools. With the exception of the married diaconate, none of these reforms achieved similar support from the hierarchy. While 58 per cent of the hierarchy advocated some form of due process, only 32 per cent were in favor of small group parishes, 43 per cent in favor of the election of the pope by the Synod of Bishops, 24 per cent favored the election of bishops by priests, and 39 per cent agreed that some married priests might work in a variety of ministries. While it may be

a matter of some surprise that as many as two fifths of the bishops were dissatisfied with the present means of electing the pope, and one quarter with the present means of electing bishops, it is nonetheless quite clear that most of the reforms which are considered important by the overwhelming majority of priests are not considered important by most bishops.

9. The strongest dissatisfaction with the distribution of power in the institutional structure of the Church is to be found in the young clergy, and this difference is rooted apparently in their very different values about the nature of the Church and the nature of Christianity. What is happening is not merely a disagreement between those who have power and those who do not; it is a disagreement among those with opposing ideologies about the nature of the reality whose power structure is the subject of disagreement. In other words, the power conflict in the Church is rooted in ideological differences, a fact which is likely to exacerbate the intensity of the conflict.

SPECULATIONS

1. One would have to read the complete text and inspect all the tables of *American Priests* to realize the full extent of the differences between bishops and priests. For example, 36 per cent of the bishops and 88 per cent of the diocesan priests think that the bishop has the most influence and the most authority in appointing pastors. Eighty-four per cent of the bishops think this is the way it should be, but only 51 per cent of the active priests (24 per cent of those under thirty-five and 39 per cent of those between thirty-six and forty-five) think that this is the way things should be. Similarly, 67 per cent of the bishops and 72 per cent of the diocesan priests think that the bishop has in fact the principal authority in the assignment of a priest. The same percentage of bishops (67 per cent) think this is the way things should be, while only 41 per cent of the diocesan priests think it is the way things

should be, as do only 16 per cent of the priests under thirty-five and 30 per cent of those between thirty-six and forty-five. Fifty-three per cent of the bishops think that the priests should have a great deal of power in the diocese and 50 per cent of them think that they actually do have a great deal of power. On the other hand, 61 per cent of the diocesan priests think that they should have a great deal of power, and only 23 per cent of them think that they do in fact have a great deal of power. Bishops, in other words, are satisfied with the role the priests have, priests are not satisfied with it.

These examples, while not chosen exactly randomly, are none-theless typical of differences which extend to almost every area under consideration. It is not that priests do not want bishops to have power; indeed, 90 per cent of the diocesan priests and 88 per cent of the religious think the bishop should have a great deal of power; even 85 per cent of the priests under thirty-five think this. The problem, then, is not so much that priests want the bishops to abolish their own power as it is that they want to share more of it. The bishops, for their part, are not willing to do this, apparently feeling that they have already shared enough.

One of the results of this disagreement over the distribution of power is that priests are more likely to reject exercises of power that they find unacceptable—as we have indicated in previous chapters in commenting on the Breviary and birth control issues. In addition, they are also likely to act on their own initiative. About half the priests report that they have said Mass in a home or an apartment on their own authority, more than two fifths say that they have notably modified the rubrics of the Mass to fit the occasion, a third say they have said Mass without proper vestments, 21 per cent have said that they have given communion to non-Catholics (despite repeated prohibi-tions of such behavior), and 16 per cent say that they have given sacraments to those who are divorced and remarried. Among those under thirty-five, 40 per cent have given communion to non-Catholics, and a quarter have given the sacraments to those who are divorced and remarried. In other words, it would appear that the bishops' power to enforce their authority may be diminishing.

2. The problem of authority and structure in the Roman Catholic Church is very complicated. The ideology on which the present structure is based argues that the distribution of authority is of divine origin, that bishops are "successors to the apostles," and that they enjoy in a special way the guidance of the Holy Spirit; *a fortiori*, the pope is the vicar of Christ, the successor of Peter, and so guided by the Holy Spirit as to be infallible. Under such circumstances, the role of authority is viewed almost necessarily as a lonely and difficult one. The pope and the bishops will speak the words of Christ quite independently of what people think, or of the changing winds of popular fashion. The authority of the Church leadership is divine and sacred and it would be immoral to share this authority with others, since pope and bishops do not possess authority on their own but only as delegates from God. It is not their authority to give away and share. Whether one obtains consent and credibility is irrelevant; all that counts is that one be true to the tradition of the Church (as one interprets it oneself, of course), the promptings of the Holy Spirit, and the power that Christ has given one.

Much of this is absolute nonsense theologically, historically, psychologically, and sociologically. Father Raymond Brown has pointed out in his book, *Priest and Bishop*, that bishops are not really the successors of the apostles in the way most of them would like to imagine, and whatever the theological explanation of "infallibility" may be, such infallibility has not prevented the papacy from all kinds of disastrous mistakes both in the past and in the present. One Catholic layman remarked to me when I told him that after all the encyclical letter *Humanae Vitae* was not an exercise in infallible authority, "If infallibility doesn't apply to something that important, what the hell good is it?"

Furthermore, there is enough historical information for us to know, for example, that the Council of Basle, which in some fashion made the pope subject to review by general council, was indeed considered an authentic council in its own age and that until the early Middle Ages election of bishops by the clergy and sometimes the laity of the diocese was a matter of course. Indeed, two popes in the sixth century asserted that it was the only permissible way to select ecclesiastical leaders. Furthermore, the mechanisms of consultation in group decisions that can be found in many of the religious orders are merely modern survivals of far more democratic ecclesiastical practices that existed in the supposedly benighted Middle Ages than exist in a contemporary democratic world. One curious example of this was the Catholic University of America faculty which until recently had the privilege of electing its own dean, a practice inherited from the medieval past through the European Catholic university system. The new lay president of the Catholic University abolished this practice (by refusing to transmit to the trustees the name of Father Roland Murphy as dean of the School of Sacred Theology because he thought that Father Murphy would be objectionable to the trustees). This was done in the name of "Americanizing" the structure of the university. Interestingly enough, the medieval practice at Catholic U. was far more democratic than the practice at most other secular universities in the United States.

We know from both history and theology that there is nothing to prevent far more democratic procedures within the Church. What we have now is clearly not the only way the Church can be governed but rather a Renaissance form of absolutism which has been dressed up and sacralized by shallow theology.

Whatever the sources of their power, bishops no more than anyone else can legitimately deceive themselves into thinking that the authority of the government does not rest itself upon the consent of the governed, for if those whom you govern are not willing to accept your authority, then for all practical and effective purposes your authority is nonexistent. Until recently bishops were able to impose their authority by appeal to its presumably sacred nature. That appeal is no longer effective because priests do not think the sacredness that they agree does surround the authority of bishops and the pope applies to all matters. It does not permit ecclesiastical leadership to govern without consultation and consensus. Bishops and the pope do not yet seem to realize that this change has occurred. They continue to issue statements and proclamations appealing to the motivations of the past. In fact, however, in many dioceses all the bishop controls are the diocesan finances, and virtually every other exercise of authority either must obtain the consent of his clergy or it is largely without effect. There is absolutely no reason to think that this development will not get progressively stronger. Priests will continue to widen the area in which they demand that they be consulted and given the right to consent, and certainly this area will continue to increase until it includes virtually everything in the life of the Church. The important question is, when will the bishops recognize that such a change has taken place and begin to adjust their style of government to the new reality?

3. The fundamental issue for Church structure, it seems to me, is not sexuality but power. As we will show in later chapters, most priests think this too. The emphasis on sexuality is largely a function of the fact that the mass media find sexuality in the Roman Catholic Church to be an interminably fascinating subject. If the bishops were as cynical as I am (and I don't think many of them are), they would delight in the emphasis on sexuality because it is a peripheral issue, which as such presents no real challenge to their power. If I were a bishop interested in preserving my power, I would cheerfully support birth control and marriage for the clergy, hoping that such concessions would take priests' minds off the fact that the Church is governed by a small, self-perpetuating power elite.

4. There is, as I see it, no substitution for a reform of the method of nomination of the bishops. Unless and until this happens, the American Church is going to be in a state of increasing polarization and conflict. The bright promise and hopes of the Vatican Council will be doomed to be blighted, and the great opportunity for growth in American Catholicism will certainly be stunted. The bishops are simply not responsible to their priests and people—unless, as many of them do, they freely and consciously decide to be responsible. There is nothing in the system by which they are selected or promoted or by which they obtain great power that requires them to be in the slightest way responsive to the needs and wishes of their flocks. It is necessary only that they please Rome, the apostolic delegate, and the shadowy elite of cronies who are responsible for the selection and promotion of bishops. I am not suggesting that the American bishops are either malicious or incompetent; on the contrary, I think there is probably more talent in the American hierarchy than in any hierarchy in the world. The problem is, rather, that those who choose to exercise their talents and instinct and insight by running democratic, open-ended American dioceses are quite likely to go into the apostolic delegate's file of "unsafe" men.

The majority of the American bishops (in my own experience, the overwhelming majority) are gracious, kindly, democratic in their personal styles, and seriously concerned about the Church. Yet relatively few of them are willing to stand up to the power elite and take a vigorous and forceful role in modernizing ecclesiastical structures. For all practical purposes, a tiny handful of men, most of them only vaguely aware of what is happening in the Church, determine the policies of the American Catholic hierarchy. They impose their wishes on their colleagues by appealing to Roman authority by the prestige and power they enjoy and by the control of appointments and promotions which they have completely locked up.

5. The quality of the American hierarchy has sadly declined ever since the Vatican Council. The great leaders of the Council are now, for the most part, dead. They have been replaced, if not in their own dioceses, at least in the influential positions in the informal power structure, by men who were recommended by the Roman Curia precisely because they could be expected to slow down the pace of ecclesiastical reform. It is not merely that there are no John Irelands, Lancaster Spauldings, John Keanes, or John Englands in the American Church; there is not even a leader of the stature, influence, and vision of the late Albert Gregory Meyer. In other words, in this time of grave crisis, the leadership in the American Church is occupied by men who are adept at keeping their fences in Rome mended but who are incompetent to lead in a new situation in which the ability to obtain consent is far more important than the ability to appeal to the sacred nature of one's own power.

6. I am told by theologians that the bishop has a dual role in the Church: He speaks for the Church of God as it is manifested in a given place to the Universal Church, and he also speaks to the local church for the Church Universal. Unfortunately, in the present arrangement of power, the bishop may very well speak for the Universal Church to the local church, but there is very little he can say, at least in the normal course of events, for his own local church to the Church Universal. He was in no sense elected by the local church, and he is in no way—other than that which he might clearly choose—responsible to the local church. It is very, very difficult to speak for a group of human beings to whom you are in no way responsible. Indeed, if a bishop chooses to be responsible to his diocese so that he might accurately represent the opinions of the priests and the people in his diocese, he may run the risk of being laughed at by his colleagues in the clergy.

John Carroll, in insisting that the first American bishop be selected by his colleagues in the clergy, argued that in a country with the political style and social values of the United States this was the only appropriate way to select bishops. If such an argument could be made in 1790, it could certainly be made much more strongly in 1971. The American hierarchy is not likely to ever again obtain the consensus it once had unless nomination to its membership involves the active and meaningful participation of at least the clergy and probably, eventually, the laity too.

It is frequently said that my argument advocates the "politicization" of the Church, and I am told that all kinds of terrible things will happen when men begin to campaign for episcopal office. This is all to laugh. Only the most incredibly naïve would think that the Church is not politicized now, or indeed that any human organization can avoid politicization. Only the most ignorant can think that men do not engage in active campaigns for episcopal appointment and promotion; indeed, it was said of one very prominent American hierarch that his campaign for the office he presently holds was a brilliant and classic example of how one obtains power in the Church, a campaign begun when he was still a seminarian. The question is not whether we will have politics in the Church and in the nomination of bishops; it is rather what kind of politics will we have? Will they be the relatively open and relatively honest politics of democratic processes, or will they be the shadowy, degrading, and frequently corrupt politics of cronyism?

As Winston Churchill was alleged to have remarked, "Democracy is a terribly inefficient way of running a society—until one looks at the alternatives." The present alternative in the American Church to democracy is incredibly inefficient and growing more so.

7. As we shall note later on, if one considers the most serious problem in the American Church to be the resignation of priests, then one will not focus on structural reform, for there is nothing in our data to show that dissatisfaction with authority

by itself leads to a propensity to resign. Institutional reform will not prevent resignation, but it will likely prevent the growing polarization between clergy and hierarchy and the resultant anarchy in which leadership no longer enjoys either credibility or consensus. American priests are not anarchists or revolutionaries. Indeed, I don't think that most of them could even be called radical democrats, but they are no longer willing to concede absolute and unquestioned powers to men on whose ascent to leadership roles they have not been consulted. The dramatic changes from immigrant Church to suburb and from Counter Reformation to ecumenical age have permanently destroyed the sacred absolutism by which the Church was governed before 1960. The question is not whether the old style of power can ever reassert itself, it is, rather, whether a drastic change in the institutional structure of the Church will occur before, in the absence of leadership, American Catholicism deteriorates into complete chaos.

8. Finally, I cannot resist commenting on the rather small number of priests who advocate the closing of Catholic schools. Despite a decade of intense propaganda from liberal opinion makers, Catholic and non-Catholic, about the uselessness, the danger, and the inappropriateness of Catholic schools and about the impossibility of their continuation, practically every study that has been done shows that approximately 75 per cent of the Catholic laity in the country still support such schools. It is interesting to note from our data that only 20 per cent of the diocesan priests and 17 per cent of the active priests are in favor of the elimination of Catholic schools. "Ah," says the liberal, "it is the young priests that are against them." But neither can this stereotypical assertion be supported by the empirical data. Sixty-nine per cent of the priests under thirty-five and 77 per cent of those between thirty-six and forty-five are not willing to agree to the elimination of the Catholic school systems. So, while there is somewhat less support for Catholics schools among the young, it is nonetheless true that almost seven out of ten priests under

thirty-five are willing to support Catholic schools in one way or another—a percentage very close to that of the level of support found for parochial schools in the general Catholic population. Mythology can be very powerful, and the mythology of eroding support for Catholic schools is not likely to yield to our data, but at least it can be said that this mythology is based on what Eric Hoffer would call "true belief" and not on facts.

RECOMMENDATIONS

1. If ever the credibility and legitimacy of ecclesiastical authority is to be re-established, there must be participation first of all by the clergy and then in due time by the laity in the process of nominating bishops. I would be content for a start with a form something like that which in fact existed until the First World War: The priests of the diocese (and not just the irremovable pastors and diocesan consulters, as was the case formerly) would submit a list of three names to Rome, along with three names prepared by the bishops of the province and, if it is a major see, three names prepared by the bishops of the country. No man would then be chosen bishop unless his name appeared on the list submitted by the priests of the diocese. If Rome found all three names unsuitable, it could require that another list be prepared. This reform is, I think, a very modest first step. The involvement of the laity and religious might take place in the following election of bishops by methods to be worked out in consultation among the bishops, priests, religious, and laity of the diocese after the first democratically nominated bishop had been selected.

2. I would even be willing to settle for the institution of this modest reform of mine whenever a diocese fell vacant, without insisting that all those who are bishops now should resign to permit their successors to be nominated democratically. Nevertheless, I think it would be desirable that many bishops indicate

their support for this democratization by at least offering their resignations to the clergy of their dioceses.

3. I should also think that after the democratically nominated hierarchy was duly constituted, or at least after substantial numbers of democratically nominated bishops are represented at meetings of the hierarchy, the bishops should initiate discussion about the possibility of setting a term for service in the episcopal office. My own inclination is to think that two four- or five-year terms are the most that one can demand that any man serve in such a difficult position. More important than the length or number of terms is the recognition of the desirability of limited service, both because it gives the electorate an opportunity to review their choice and it gives the man an opportunity to escape the burdens that no man ought to impose on himself for too long a period of time.

4. Diocesan senates ought to be constituted together with pastoral councils as governing bodies of the dioceses with full legislative power, subject as are most democratic institutions to veto by the bishop. The situation of class conflict between senate and bishop is highly undesirable, and both sides should realize that while the bishop cannot govern without his senate, neither can the senate govern without its bishop. In case of conflict between the two, no solution unacceptable to either is likely to be effective.

5. Furthermore, the present "due process" system which is beginning to emerge in American dioceses should be expanded and given full independent judicial power, with all the safeguards, rights, and privileges guaranteed by that due process to the individual by American civil law extended also to ecclesiastical law.[3]

6. The same kind of reforms I am recommending for the local church should also take place in the Universal Church. The

---

[3] And the disgraceful, weakly worded, cowardly, compromising "Bill of Rights" as contained in the new Fundamental Law should be forgotten as discreetly and as charitably as possible.

pope should be elected, if not by a general council, at least by the Synod of Bishops or by duly chosen representatives of the world's hierarchy. In a later phase, the clergy, religious, and laity should also participate in elections of their leader. The Synod of Bishops should be given full legislative power and be considered an ecumenical council in miniature. (And perhaps ecumenical councils ought to be held more frequently, too.) The corrupt, incompetent system of apostolic delegates and papal nuncios should be abolished, and Rome's dealings should be directly with the presidents of the national hierarchies or the representatives of these hierarchies in Rome. The Roman Curia should be abolished, most of its functionaries pensioned off to appropriate Italian parishes and dioceses, and replaced by an international civil service that is subject to the pope and whatever legislative body comes into existence. The new civil service should be concerned with research, planning, coordination of resources, and should have no administrative or policy making authority of its own. Its function ought to be to implement the policies made jointly by the pope and the council or the international synod. The officers of the civil service should not be cardinals, bishops, or members of the international synod. Finally, most of the Roman judicial bodies should be abolished, with whatever ecclesiastical cases that remain in the Church to be decided at the local or national level. In Rome there should be merely a court of appeals, a sort of international ombudsman to which aggrieved individuals can appeal from what they argue is unfair treatment from the diocesan or national level.

7. No one imagines, I think, that these recommendations will be received with any great enthusiasm either by the present American hierarchy or by the apostolic delegate in the Roman Curia. However, the Office of the Inquisition, the apostolic delegate, and, increasingly, the American hierarchy are becoming anachronisms; they have no real power to obtain consent, and enjoy ever decreasing credibility and legitimacy with those who are supposed to be subject to them. I do not think that the kinds

of reforms I described are going to be conceded at either the Roman or the national level. What is worse, I do not think that pressure will be strong enough to force such reforms; most American clergy, and laity too, for that matter, are going to go their own ways and do their own things and ignore the institutional structure of the Church. In some ways this may be a healthy attitude, since the fixation on ecclesiastical structure which has marked so much of the agitation and discussion of the last half decade may be unhealthy, indeed, even a sign on how dependent we still are on the father figure symbol out of the past. I do not think, though, that over the long haul the Church can do without structure any more than can any human organization, and eventually it will be reformed, either under great pressure or upon the complete collapse of its credibility and legitimacy. The result of the latter will be a long period of chaos during which, slowly and painfully, new administrative organizational and governmental structures will begin to emerge. I see absolutely no reason to think that the latter alternative is not what is going to happen. As with mysticism and celibacy, American Catholicism will have to rediscover at great cost and considerable suffering the advantages of effective organizational structure. In the meantime, the Church which successfully adjusted to American society while resisting the onslaughts of the Know-Nothings, the Nativists, the APA (American Protective Association), and the Ku Klux Klan can be seen tearing itself apart just at the moment when it has finally been fully accepted as part of American society. Non-Catholic observers will stand by in a combination of horror and fascinated delight as we come apart at the seams. They would be mistaken, however, to write us off; Catholicism has managed to rebound before from its own disastrous mistakes, though such rebounds are usually measured in terms of centuries.

8

PRIESTS AT WORK

FINDINGS

1. Most priests work moderately long hours—in excess of fifty hours per week. Religious priests are more satisfied with their jobs than diocesan priests. Older priests are in general more satisfied with their jobs than younger priests. Job satisfactions of associate pastors are not only lower than other priests, they are also lower than those of unskilled American industrial workers, for example.

2. Despite their problems, priests compare themselves favorably with other professionals, such as doctors and lawyers on the general characteristics of professionalism.

3. Although the majority of American priests see themselves in need of and interested in professional updating, many of them are rather regular readers of serious authors and journals.

4. The highest levels of job satisfaction are to be found among those who do writing and research or are in some kind of higher educational work, either in major seminaries, university and college teaching, educational administration, or campus ministry. The lowest levels of satisfaction are to be found among high school and grade school teachers, those whose principal work is religious instruction, those who are in parish work, and those whose work is concerned with the arts. Middle levels of satisfaction exist for religious and diocesan administrators,

chancery office officials, institutional chaplains, and those engaged in social work and counseling.

5. Eighty-three per cent of the diocesan priests and 46 per cent of the religious order priests report that parish work is among their current main jobs. Second on the list checked by parish priests is high school and grade school teaching, which is mentioned by 18 per cent. The second most important job current for religious priests is counseling, as mentioned by 25 per cent; third is high school and grade school teaching (17 per cent); and fourth is university and college teaching (14 per cent). Counseling (16 per cent) is third for diocesan priests; and religious instruction (14 per cent) is the fourth most frequently mentioned current main job. One concludes, therefore, that those kinds of jobs which provide the lowest levels of satisfaction are also the ones in which most priests find themselves spending most of their time.

6. We have avoided the use of statistical tables in this book, but the accompanying one provides some indication of the reaction of the various age groups of priests to their occupational experience. It is worth inspecting, I think. The overwhelming majority of priests would enter the priesthood again, and while there is some correlation with age, three quarters of those under thirty-five would do it again. Interestingly enough, the percentage is somewhat lower (71 per cent) for those between thirty-six and forty-five. However, at no age level are a majority willing to assert that they feel their talents are being used a great deal. Large majorities consider that they compare favorably with other professionals in both their depth of knowledge and skill in their commitment to serving the needs of people. A substantial majority also thinks that priests compare to other professionals in having responsibility for an undertaking. There is a correlation with age on this matter, though; young priests are less likely than older priests to compare themselves favorably with other professionals. That characteristic of the professional which is least likely to be the object of favorable comparisons by

priests is "autonomy to make decisions," though only among those under thirty-five do less than half say that they have about as much if not more autonomy than do other professionals.

TABLE I   JOB REACTIONS BY AGE
(Per Cent of Active Diocesan and Religious Priests)

Reactions	Age			
	26–35	36–45	46–55	Over 55
Would enter priesthood again	74	71	80	89
Feel talents are utilized "a great deal"	26	38	44	47
More or about the same as other professionals:				
Depth of knowledge and skill	71	76	79	79
Autonomy to make decisions	45	52	65	68
Responsibility for an undertaking	64	71	79	83
Commitment to serving needs of people	92	93	92	90

7. Two thirds of the priests feel they need more study to convey Christian faith to a rapidly changing society, and three fifths say they need updating in biblical, theological, and related fields. Interestingly enough, the proportion drops to two fifths who want further training in ministerial skills (preaching, counseling, etc.) and a little more than one third who want to learn how to be a change agent in Church and community. In other words, clergy seem to recognize that their deficiencies are in the area of theory rather than practice, a recognition which is found even among the clergy under thirty-five.

8. Substantial proportions of priests keep in touch with the Catholic periodical literature. All active clergy list their local diocesan newspaper as the publication they read the most. Among the bishops the next most popular journals are *The Priest* (54 per cent), *America* (52 per cent), and *Worship* (36 per cent). The other most popular journals among active dioc-

esan priests are *The National Catholic Reporter* (40 per cent), *The Priest* (31 per cent), *Homiletic and Pastoral Review* (25 per cent), *America* (24 per cent), and *The Critic* (22 per cent). Major superiors vote for *The National Catholic Reporter* (51 per cent), *America* (42 per cent), *The Priest* (30 per cent, *The Critic* and *Homiletic and Pastoral Review* (29 per cent each), and *Theological Studies* (21 per cent). Active religious priests also give top billing to *The National Catholic Reporter* (39 per cent), followed by *America* (28 per cent), *The Critic* and *Homiletic and Pastoral Review* (21 per cent each), and *The Priest* (19 per cent). The "liberal" journal *Commonweal* is read by 15 per cent among both the diocesan and the religious priests, and the "conservative" *The Wanderer* is read by 8 per cent of the diocesan and 6 per cent of the religious priests. It is interesting to note that with the exception of *The National Catholic Reporter* and *The Critic*, the bishops are more likely to report reading every one of the journals listed than are the active diocesan priests. Perhaps the episcopal office involves some sense of responsibility that one ought to "keep up" with as much Catholic periodical literature as possible.

Most of the journals mentioned above would be characterized as "middlebrow," but *Theology Digest, Theological Studies, Concilium,* and *The Catholic Biblical Quarterly* are serious scholarly journals, and one tenth of the American Catholic priests report that they read most issues of these magazines. There are no data available on the reading of professional journals by members of other professions, but one must say on the basis of our research that one would be hard put to make a case against the proposition that important segments of the Catholic clergy do indeed strive to keep abreast of current developments in their profession.

Among the young clergy, *The National Catholic Reporter* continues to be the most popular journal (54 per cent) after the local diocesan newspaper. *The Critic* (31 per cent) takes second place, followed by *America* (24 per cent) and *Commonweal*

(20 per cent). Among priests over fifty-five, *The Priest* is the most frequently mentioned journal (39 per cent), followed by *Homiletic and Pastoral Review* (36 per cent), *America* (26 per cent), and *The National Catholic Reporter* (22 per cent). The younger clergy and the older clergy seem to read rather different journals. *Commonweal*, for example, is twice as popular among the younger clergy, as is *The National Catholic Reporter*. *America*, on the other hand, is read by approximately one quarter of all age groups.

9. There is also considerable interest among Catholic priests in some of the more important Catholic writers of the last decade. If one notes in passing the fact that the overwhelming majority of priests and bishops alike report themselves as "greatly influenced" by the documents of Vatican II, and if one also notes the importance of the writings of Paul VI to all categories of active clergy, then one can say that for the bishops the most popular of the theological writers is Karl Rahner (41 per cent) and the second most popular is the great American theologian John Courtney Murray (36 per cent). Twenty-three per cent of the bishops mention Cardinal Bea as having greatly influenced their thinking, and 20 per cent mention both Jacques Maritain and Cardinal Suenens of Brussels. Active diocesan priests are most likely to report that they were influenced by the European theologian Bernard Haring (29 per cent) and the American psychologist Eugene Kennedy (28 per cent). Other popular authors with the diocesan clergy are John L. McKenzie (26 per cent), Karl Rahner (26 per cent), Louis Evely (24 per cent), Edward Schillebeeckx (24 per cent), Teilhard de Chardin (23 per cent), and Hans Küng (23 per cent). Karl Rahner is the most popular of the influential authors among the major superiors (36 per cent) and among active religious priests (32 per cent).

Among the clergy thirty-five and under, Bernard Haring leads the list (49 per cent), but 41 per cent of the young clergy reported that they were greatly influenced by Teilhard de Chardin and Eugene Kennedy, and about 35 per cent reported that they were influenced by Louis Evely, Hans Küng, and John L. McKenzie. The Catholic writers read most infrequently by all groups are Daniel Callahan (4 per cent by the youngest priests) and Rosemarie Reuther (2 per cent by the youngest priests).

Rahner, Schillebeeckx, Küng, Haring, and Cardinal Suenens are some of the most important European leaders of the intellectual movements in the Church since the Vatican Council. Murray, McKenzie, and Kennedy are major intellectual figures in the American Catholic environment. The fact that considerable proportions of the American priesthood are willing to say that these writers have greatly influenced their thinking indicates that very serious effort has been put into the attempt to keep up with the most recent developments in the Church. About one tenth of the priests over fifty-five, for example, say that they have been greatly influenced by the work of Cardinal Suenens, and one fifth of these older priests say the same thing about Karl Rahner. Given the extreme depth and complexity of Professor Rahner's thought, one is forced to conclude that those older priests who have pursued his work vigorously enough to be greatly influenced by him have shown an impressive level of professional commitment.

SPECULATIONS

1. Since we do not have comparable data on other professional groups, it is impossible to say how well the American clergy would compare in their professional standards with other groups. Nevertheless, there is nothing in the data presented in the previous section that would lead us to say that the clergy look unimpressive. They work moderately long hours and evaluate themselves rather highly in comparison with other professional groups. Substantial proportions of them keep in contact with the periodical literature in their field and read the most serious and most important professional scholars. The majority of them are

aware of the need to update their professional skills. Whether the counterparts of Karl Rahner would be as popular in other professions and whether journals such as *Concilium* would be as widely read cannot be estimated with absolute confidence, but until data become available, it can be safely said that the professionalism of the Catholic clergy looks quite good in absolute terms.

2. Indeed, one is struck by the fact that they are able to maintain such high standards in the face of fairly low levels of job satisfaction. While the job satisfaction of priests—as, say, for associate pastors—compares favorably enough with those of typical American males, it is nonetheless interesting that less than half report that they feel their talents are challenged "a great deal" in their occupational responsibilities. A low level of job satisfaction correlates somewhat with the propensity to resign from the priesthood, but a correlation of .23 is not very high. Furthermore, while associate pastors are less likely to enjoy job satisfaction than are other members of the clergy, correlations between being an associate pastor and job satisfaction is less than —.2, and hence does not rate a place in the causal model we will propound in a later chapter. In fact, job satisfaction is explained only to a very minor extent by the kind of work one does, and even less by the sort of structural situation in which one finds oneself. Our explanatory causal model is only able to explain 6 per cent of the variants on the job satisfaction index, with family tension contributing 2 per cent of the explanation, inner-directed personality, 2 per cent more, and religious experience, the final 2 per cent. In other words, those with more serene family backgrounds, those with inner-directed personalities, and those who had experienced the presence of God were more likely to be satisfied on their jobs than those from tense families or with low inner-directed and religious experience scores. It is notable that none of these is a structural variable; they are, rather, social-psychological variables; and they leave the question of why some people are satisfied with their

work in the priesthood and others are not largely unanswered. We are forced to conclude that whether a priest is satisfied in his work or not is probably the result of personality variables that we have not been able to measure with the POI scale; it is not the result of institutional variations.

3. We are able to do somewhat better in explaining how priests rated themselves in comparison to other professionals. Once again, structural or occupational variables were not pertinent, and family tension, religious experience, personality (as measured by the POI), age, and adherence to traditional religious values were the most likely predictors of a high self-evaluation as a professional.

4. The point must be emphasized once again so that it will not be missed: As desirable as institutional reform may be in the Church, there is no evidence in our data that it will necessarily improve either the work satisfaction or the professional comparison scores of American priests. Presumably, ways could be found to make the work more challenging and exciting, so that higher levels of satisfaction could be achieved; there is a positive correlation between work satisfaction and both the number of hours worked per week and the feeling that one's talents are being challenged "a great deal." In other words, those who work longer hours are likely to be more satisfied with their job, and those who feel that there are constant challenging demands being made on them are also likely to feel satisfied with their jobs. If one wishes to improve the occupational satisfaction of priests, it would seem that one must give them more to do and make more challenging demands on them. It is perhaps an interesting group of human professionals who seem to want more work rather than less.

5. Generally speaking, priests compare themselves favorably with other professions, but it is true that the least favorable of comparisons have to do with matters of individual autonomy and responsibility. The associate pastor has a level of job satisfaction lower than that of a manual worker in American indus-

try. Improvement of job satisfaction for associate pastors and the expansion of opportunities for authority, responsibility, and autonomy among all priests is not likely—at least as far as we can tell from our analysis—to lower resignation rates substantially. (There are other and far more powerful predictors of the propensity to resign.) It is nonetheless true that reforms might notably improve the effectiveness of priests in their work.

Much of the training we received in the seminary emphasized obedience and docility; we were to respond rather than initiate, react rather than act, wait for work and/or people to come to us rather than seeking it. The good associate pastor was the man who did what he was told. (He might on occasion make a discreet and respectful suggestion to his pastor.) Obedience, we were assured, was the most difficult and the most important of the priestly virtues. (That it was more difficult to attain than "purity" was stated explicitly; that it was more important than zeal or charity was strongly implied.) In large, urban dioceses where men remained associate pastors for most of their lives, there were in most parishes relatively little opportunity to exercise initiative and responsibility. In the drastic changes that have occurred in the Church in the last decade, this situation, I think, may have been substantially changed. In many dioceses the power of the bishop to restrain pastors from doing what they want and the power of pastors to restrain associate pastors from doing what they want has been notably weakened if not completely eliminated. While "authority" is the most frequently mentioned serious problem of priests (as we shall investigate in another chapter), it does not seem to be authority as represented by one's immediate local superior; it is rather authority on a more general, structural, and perhaps even abstract and theoretical level. As we shall see in the next chapter, most priests as well as most religious report rather good relationships with the one in charge of the house in which they live. One may speculate, at least, that in the average day-to-day life of a priest, the problem is now no longer obtaining enough freedom to act on one's own initiative and responsibility as in knowing what to do with the freedom one already possesses. As I understand the findings of the Loyola psychological research, these scholars seem to be making the same point. I am not suggesting that dissatisfaction with authority or with structure is all projection. There are institutions in the Church which technically may still be oppressive, and they do not create the positive environment in which freedom may be enjoyed and initiative exercised. I am suggesting, however, that it seems to me to be altogether possible that it is no longer true that the associate pastor is the only remnant of medieval serfdom still surviving. (A suggestion I made five years ago.) The question may not be how do serfs free themselves, but what do serfs do when the authority structure that maintained their servility has collapsed around them.

6. There is a certain blandness in our findings about professionalism and job satisfaction. Priests are not terribly dissatisfied with their work, nor do they seem to be terribly excited by it. Work satisfaction plays only a relatively minor role in their staying in the priesthood or in their resigning from it. They certainly do not compare themselves unfavorably with other professionals in terms of their initiative, autonomy, and responsibility, though they did not give themselves quite as high ratings on these matters as they did on their training and commitment. They work moderately long hours, but do not feel themselves greatly challenged. They keep up with the professional literature, but need more updating of professional skills, particularly theoretical ones. All of this leads me to conclude that while considerable experimentation is certainly appropriate to improve the effectiveness of the work of the American priests and to provide greater job satisfactions for them, it would be a mistake to assume that such experimentation by itself will create a situation in which people are less likely to resign from the ministry. Nor does it seem to me that one can even be sure any longer that such experimentation is required in order to provide

priests with the amount of freedom they need to do their professional work. I think that challenge is more important to them than freedom.

Perhaps at no other part of our survey is the lack of information on lay attitudes such a crucial weakness in our search for understanding. One would at this point desperately like to know what the laity think of the professionalism and the occupational performance of the clergy, and what kinds of reform they would like to have in order to improve service rendered to them by their priests.

7. As both a social scientist and a priest committed to change, I enthusiastically endorse experimental ministries, but I would hope that these ministries be experimental. If there are no previously established criteria of success or failure, then what is taking place cannot be called an experiment; merely an innovation. One has no way of knowing whether one innovation is more or less effective in achieving a desired goal than those techniques it replaces. Sometimes one has the impression that in certain kinds of innovative ministries if the team does not break up in conflict or if its members do not leave the priesthood to marry the female members of the team or the local sister superior, then the innovation is proclaimed a success. Any innovation without clearly defined norms by which success or failure can be measured as well as clearly outlined procedures for outside evaluation is irresponsible.

Furthermore, I would hope that very careful screening is practiced in selecting for innovative ministries. By definition, innovation departs from the ordinary; if the innovation has any chance of working at all, it will require people who are mature and stable enough to maintain their poise and their integrity in new, unfamiliar, and frequently disorienting situations. Unfortunately, I have the impression that ministerial innovations are frequently staffed by precisely the kind of person who volunteers for innovation in order that he may escape from his own emotional problems. If he is permitted to work out his emotional difficulties in an "experimental" environment, two things are likely to happen: (1) He will not work them out, and (2) in the attempt, he is likely to destroy the experiment—and perhaps impose severe handicaps on the lay people he is allegedly serving.

Thus, those who are responsible for programing and evaluating experimental ministries ought to be very careful about who is chosen to staff such experiments. It may well be a legitimate strategy to turn over some experimental situations to noisy, troubled malcontents as a technique for "cooling them off." If such an admittedly cynical strategy is going to be followed, let it be clear to those who are responsible for evaluating the program that what is happening has nothing to do with experimentation or innovation.

Finally, I would certainly hope that the advice and consent of the laity, who are to be the objects of an experimental ministry, be sought. I have the impression that not infrequently innovations are imposed on lay people who have not been asked about whether they want to be the object of experimentation and who are given no choice but to accept what the experimenters have in mind. What I find especially surprising and reprehensible about this technique is that it seems to be practiced often precisely by those clergy who are the loudest in proclaiming their own liberalism and their own commitment to lay participation. I have the impression that what they mean by lay participation is the participation of those lay people who happen to share their values. I think if the right to advise and consent is conceded only to those who agree with one or only to those who happen to merit it, then it is no right at all, only a privilege.

RECOMMENDATIONS

1. Research on the laity's reaction to the work of the clergy is absolutely imperative, and such a research project, hopefully

funded jointly by bishop and priest organizations, ought to begin at once. It won't, of course, but it still ought to.

2. Offices of experimentation ought to be established in both dioceses and religious communities. They should promote, monitor, evaluate, and summarize experimental ministries, and make recommendations both about the continuation of experimentation and directions for new experimentation. It should be established clearly that no one has a right to introduce an innovation on his own without consulting both his lay and clerical colleagues, at least to the extent that innovation may impinge on the well-being of these colleagues and on their spheres of action.

3. In addition to personnel boards and due process units which are increasingly widespread in American dioceses and orders, there also ought to be ethical practices committees, which would establish appropriate standards of behavior for priests either in experimental or traditional ministries and be authorized to sanction violations of these ethical standards. There has been a considerable increase in the amount of freedom and rights of the clergy vis-à-vis their superiors without a corresponding increase in the freedom and rights of the laity vis-à-vis the clergy. A man certainly has the prerogative of doing his own thing, but he must do it, one would assume, within the context of the responsibilities of the profession he has embraced, or run the risk of being temporarily or permanently suspended from that profession. Most priests, I would hazard, are very responsible in discharging their professional obligations, but it would not be surprising in time of change and chaos if some men interpreted their newfound freedom as the right to do absolutely anything they pleased to do so. It is increasingly difficult for bishops to impose sanctions on these men (though it was perhaps never quite as easy as the clergy themselves may have believed. What, after all, does a bishop do to someone who refuses to work?). As a result the laity really have no protection from a lazy, rude, irresponsible, immature cleric; neither do his colleagues who are forced

to work with him. Like every other group of professional men, the clergy must establish standards and mechanisms with which to police themselves or run the risk eventually of having one's clients or the larger society impose standards whether one likes them or not.

4. I deliberately chose to recommend ethical practices committees before I make the recommendation in this section that priests be given the maximum amount of freedom to develop their talents and exercise their initiative and responsibility. I wish to emphasize that this recommendation for maximizing talent and initiative is not intended to imply that priests are excused from the responsibilities of their ministry. I am well aware that the overwhelming majority of priests would not infer from a demand for increased personal development and increased personal initiative that a means for escaping responsibility is intended. That many Church leaders chose to interpret such demands that way and can find some justification for their interpretation in the occasional behavior of some priests is unfortunate.

Personal initiative also means personal responsibility not only to make one's own decisions but also to fulfill the obligation one has to one's role opposites. It is perhaps a hackneyed phrase, but if a priest is supposed to be "responsible for," he must also be "responsible to" his colleagues, his clients, and the leaders of the Church.

But if constraints of professional (and in this case, religious) responsibility can set up a context for the exercise of personal initiative, it does not follow that initiative and the development of one's personality are of secondary moment. On the contrary, the maximization of the talents and initiative of one's skilled professional staff is not merely something that is ethically desirable for an organization; it is an absolute functional necessity. No human organization can expect to work with any effectiveness at all if it is not making the maximum possible use of the talents and abilities of its membership, and particularly its trained, committed, full-time functionaries. The most important question for ecclesiastical leadership is not how to balance personal development with organizational responsibility (this is an important question and a difficult question, but a secondary one); the critical question, rather, is how talent and initiative can be maximized for the good of the whole organization and all of its members. The real problem in the American Church is not that some priests behave irresponsibly, but that a large number of priests do not feel adequately challenged, and that many of us are never given the opportunity to develop our potentialities and talents the way we might have.

I do not know who will address himself to this problem. Most priest organizations seem to be much too busy denouncing episcopal father figures and demanding immediate changes in the celibacy rules. The hierarchy seems to be too busy scapegoating the clergy for the problems of the Church and refusing to discuss the celibacy issue. Obviously, some bishops and many priests are concerned with the problem of the maximization of talent and responsibility, but it does not seem that the issue is very high on most agendas, and the result is that one more step is taken into the abyss of chaos.

5. With that genius for the peripheral that marks the adolescent, American Catholicism has been deeply concerned with such things as clerical clothes, clerical shelter, and clerical salary. I wear the Roman collar most of the time in the secular university environment not because I am afraid to lay aside my clerical protection but because I feel the Roman collar has some sign value at the University of Chicago, and sociologist that I am, I am well aware of the importance of religious symbolism. I live in a rectory not because I think it is the only place priests should live but because I would find an apartment of my own appallingly lonely. I accept a pay check from the University of Chicago because there are many useful and enjoyable things one can do with an extra shrinking American dollar or two. But I would not attempt to generalize from my

own solutions to the questions of clothes, housing, and money to solutions that would be appropriate for everyone else. I think we have long since left behind the situation in which ecclesiastical authority could or was even especially interested in imposing stylistic uniformity on the clergy and religious. However, if religious authority no longer is to impose a uniform style on us, then neither is anyone else, and I will not accept anyone's right to criticize me for being so old-fashioned as to wear the collar or live in a rectory or to be so greedy (or so fortunate) to be on the payroll of the National Opinion Research Center—a payroll, I might add, that has not always been easy to meet. There may very well be standards of dress, housing, and behavior that an ethical practices committee may wish to establish for priests. There also may be perhaps more important standards that good taste could dictate. (That clerical teenybopper who seems to be on Rush Street or Old Town night-club circuit almost every evening of the week is violating good taste and common sense more than anything else. One cannot abolish him by law and shouldn't have to, but a suggestion from an ethical practices committee might be effective.) Priests should make their own decisions on these matters within an overall context of responsibility to the profession and to the gospel which we are all committed to proclaim. It is also a professional obligation to realize that these issues are trivial; and the clergyman who spends a great deal of time wondering about whether he ought to wear a business suit and who thinks he has become sort of a revolutionary because he shocks his parishioners by appearing in the back of the church on Sunday morning in a tie has a great deal of maturation ahead of him.

6. My colleagues and I were greatly impressed by the quality of clerical reading and the statement of the need for more training, particularly for training in religious theory. I would therefore urge every diocese and religious community to establish regular provisions for in-service educational experiences for priests. It is important to make a distinction between two kinds

of postordination education: professional training and dilettante education. I am not using the word "dilettante" in the pejorative sense. Quite the contrary; any well-educated and civilized human being has something of the dilettante about him. If a priest wants to take courses in Indian pottery, medieval French literature, seventeenth-century English folk songs, or contemporary American mystery stories, we should warmly applaud his desire to develop and enrich his personality. But dilettantism, however praiseworthy, ought not to be confused with professional training. If one wishes to learn how to be a counselor or a religious educator or learn more about modern scripture studies or sociology so that one may use these skills in one's work, then one's training ought to be professional, which is not to say necessarily that it ought to be oriented toward the Ph.D., but that it should be part of some kind of coherent program at the end of which one possesses some skill mastery one lacked before. There is a tendency for some priests to approach theology and psychology in particular (which I take to be professional disciplines especially pertinent to the priest) as dilettantes and not as professionals. A little bit of psychology is a very dangerous thing, and a little bit of understanding of new theology or new scripture studies is equally dangerous. The Church cannot prevent, of course, someone approaching psychology and theology superficially, but at least the Church can set up programs where it is possible for those who wish to achieve some kind of competence in these disciplines—even if it is a pastoral rather than a scholarly competence—can do so relatively easily. Under such circumstances, the temptation to be a therapeutic or theological dilettante would be substantially reduced.

Obviously, we do not have much in the way of resources for setting up such in-service training programs. It must be admitted that some of the programs already in existence leave much to be desired both in the skill and in the personal maturity of those who administer and staff them.[1] Probably a consolidation of efforts through regional centers of in-service training would be appropriate, though it might require a level of co-operation between dioceses and religious communities seldom achieved in the American Church.

To conclude this chapter, amateurism is one of the grave weaknesses of American Catholicism while at the same time being one of its greatest strengths. The impressive innovations, for example, that took place in the Archdiocese of Chicago before the Vatican Council under the administrations of Cardinals Stritch and Meyer were carried on by an extraordinarily ingenious group of amateurs who established models for the whole Church and anticipated perhaps more than anything else in the United States the direction upon which the Vatican Council would thrust us. If these men had not been open-ended, flexible, free-wheeling, practically oriented amateurs, we never would have had Cana, or the Christian Family Movement, or the catechisms of Gerard Weber and James Killgallon, or the almost endless stream of creative innovations of John Egan, or the brilliant improvisations of Leo Mahon in Central America. It is only to repeat the wisdom of these men to say that they always desperately felt the need of richer and deeper theory and of more sophisticated scholarship. I would hate to see us become so professional and so scholarly that there would be no room in the American Church for the Mahons or the Egans of the future, but the taste, the instinct, and the personal wisdom of such "amateur" innovators prevented them from ever confusing their brilliant ad hoc improvisations with definitive theory. Unfortunately, in the changed set of circumstances in which we now find ourselves, it is all too easy to confuse amateurism with professionalism. Trained professionals as well as elaborated theory are in such desperate shortage. The dif-

[1] Some of the summer institutes around the country have served principally as marriage markets for people about to depart from the priesthood and the religious life; given the amateurism of the people who staff such institutes, it is not surprising that they accomplish little more.

ference between some of today's amateurs and the innovators of the Chicago school is that the latter knew they were amateurs and were constantly looking for professionalism; today, it seems that when men with Master's degrees in counseling and guidance consider themselves licensed to practice therapy, the danger is that the amateurs think they are professionals.

Amateurism may be sufficient for an immigrant post-Tridentine Church; it is not sufficient for an upper middle-class post-Vatican Church, and the only way that amateurism which thinks itself professional can be exorcised from the American Church is by the growth of real professionalism. We must increase the number of priests who are fully trained, competent practitioners with the particular skills they are required to exercise. There is, I think, an increase of professionalism of this sort among the American clergy, but I am doubtful that the increase is rapid enough to meet both the dangers and the opportunities of the present situation.

9

FRIENDSHIP, SATISFACTION, AND PROBLEMS

FINDINGS

1. While some priests by their own admission have rather few friends, most see themselves as having close personal friends, and a substantial proportion see themselves as having many such friends, some even among the laity. We will defer to the Loyola study any evaluation of the capacity of the clergy for intimate friendships; we will hazard the guess, however, on the basis of our data that the capacity for friendship, indeed the actual possession of intimate friends, is probably no less among the clergy than it is in any comparable group of adult males—it may even be greater.

2. Furthermore, even though the closest friends and most frequent associates of most priests tend to be other priests, the majority of priests claim also to have close friends who are laymen and laywomen. Unquestionably, there is a clerical life style which tends to limit interaction to other priests or to those lay people who are most likely to be favorably disposed to the clerical life style. Whether this life style is substantially more narrow and closed than that of the medical or legal professions is a question that cannot be answered on the basis of our data, though I would be surprised if the clerical culture was substantially more parochial than the legal or medical cultures.

3. Only very small minorities of priests living in parish settings describe their relationships with their colleagues as "poor" or "very poor." The accompanying table demonstrates that substantial minorities are willing to rate their colleague relationships as "excellent."

TABLE I   RELATIONS WITH COLLEAGUES
IN PARISH SETTING, BY CLERICAL STATUS
(Per Cent of Active Diocesan Priests Having Personal
Relationships with Each Type of Colleague)

Colleague	Personal relationships	
	Excellent	Poor or very poor
Pastor	30	15
Assistant(s)	43	3
Fellow assistant(s)	37	4
Resident priest(s)	37	4
Housekeeper/cook	34	4

There are only weak correlations between age and satisfaction with colleague relationships (.22 between age and colleague satisfaction). If anything, as Table 1 shows, those living in religious communities are even more likely to say they have good relationships with the person in charge and less likely to say these relationships are "poor" or "very poor" than are diocesan priests. Finally, three quarters of the diocesan priests, four fifths of the religious, and approximately two thirds of the priests under thirty-five say that they consider the place where they live to be a "home," that is to say, "a place where you can be yourself, relax, or entertain if you wish." One must conclude that only a small minority of priests find their living situations and colleague relationships intolerable.

4. The most frequently mentioned "great problem" for priests is the way authority is used in the Church (29 per cent of diocesan priests mention this); the second most frequently mentioned problem is the difficulty of reaching people (17 per cent); and the third is the loneliness of the priestly life (16 per cent). The fourth most frequently mentioned problem for diocesan priests is relationships with superiors or pastors (15 per cent); and then in fifth place a great problem for 12 per cent of the diocesan priests is celibacy. Among religious priests, celibacy is the fourth most frequently mentioned problem checked by 9 per cent of the respondents. Approximately one tenth of the priests in the country mentioned as one of the great problems the lack of opportunity for personal fulfillment, irrelevance of the work priests do, and too much work.

5. The most serious problem for priests under thirty-five is also authority, which is mentioned by 44 per cent of them. While celibacy is more likely to be mentioned as a problem by the priests under thirty-five than it is by older priests (18 per cent list it as a great problem), it is still in fifth place on their list of problems too.

6. One of the most interesting aspects of this list of problems is that loneliness, which is the third most frequently listed problem, is the strongest predictor of resignations in the priesthood, and the one we will use in a subsequent chapter in our causal model to explain why people resign. Priests are almost twice as likely to mention authority as a problem than they are to mention loneliness, but it is loneliness that predicts more strongly the propensity to leave the priesthood.

The greatest satisfactions to be found in the priesthood are the administration of the sacraments and the liturgy (83 per cent), working with people (73 per cent), and being a part of a community of Christians (60 per cent). A little less than half the priests also mention obtaining great satisfaction from the opportunity to exercise intellectual and creative abilities, the spiritual security that results from divine call, and the challenge of being a leader of the Christian community.

Not surprisingly, those who have resigned from the priesthood are less likely than the active priests to report satisfying experiences when they were in the ministry. Not only do they have fewer sources of satisfaction, they found less reward in precisely those things which most active priests find rewarding and also where most active priests must spend most of their time. Furthermore, we were most likely to find satisfaction in precisely those things such as social reform that most active priests are less likely to have the time to pursue. To put the matter somewhat differently, the resignees got less satisfaction than active priests from the religious and spiritual dimensions of the priestly role and more satisfactions from the social, intellectual, and cultural aspects of the role.

7. In this matter, the resignees were different even from the youngest members of the active clergy. Thus while priests thirty-five and under are less likely than older priests to report satisfactions from the liturgy (75 per cent as opposed to 88 per cent of those over fifty-five), they are still 21 percentage points more likely than the resignees to report liturgy and sacraments as a source of satisfaction. The younger clergy are also more likely than the resignees (and also more likely than the older clergy) to say they get satisfaction out of working with people, working with a Christian community, and serving as a leader of a Christian community. Only on the matter of social reform are the resignees more likely than the clergy under thirty-five to report more satisfaction. Thus even the younger clergy achieve greater satisfaction out of the cultic and ministerial aspects of the priesthood than resignees did, and only in the matter of social reform are resignees more likely to recall greater satisfaction.

8. Loneliness, which seems to have the greatest impact on propensity to resign, is most likely to be found in young priests,

among those with less work satisfaction, among those with less frequent religious experiences, and among those who come from strained family backgrounds. We are able to explain with our causal model about 25 per cent of the variants on the loneliness question—a question which simply asks whether loneliness is "a great problem, very little of a problem, or no problem at all." Given the crude nature of the loneliness measure, a .6 explanatory power is rather impressive. However (and this is something of a disappointment to us), there was no important relationship between scores on the POI scales and the experience of loneliness as a problem.

9. There is only a relatively moderate net effect of work satisfaction on loneliness—a beta relationship of —.21. This would suggest that if we are able to increase the amount of work satisfaction among the clergy, we would only be able to create a moderate decline in the amount of loneliness experienced in the priestly life.

10. Because of the causal design of our research, it is impossible to say whether a problem of loneliness leads to a problem of authority or vice versa. However, as we shall note in discussing our causal model in a subsequent chapter, when the mutual influence of loneliness and problems with authority are held constant, loneliness contributes much more of an explanation to desire to marry than does authority. In other words, problems with authority *by themselves* do not have much influence on either the desire to marry or the inclination to resign from the priesthood. But problems of loneliness *by themselves* do have a strong relationship both with loneliness and the subsequent desire to marry.

SPECULATIONS

1. It is fashionable for some priests to feel sorry for themselves on the grounds that their Church and their seminary experiences severely inhibited their capacity to develop intimate

friendships. Our data certainly show that most priests, at least in response to a survey questionnaire, would not be inclined to describe themselves as not having any intimate relationships. Furthermore, the personality test (POI) indicates that priests do not have an abnormally low capacity for intimacy. Our colleagues in the Loyola project did discover among many priests low levels of capacity for deep and lasting friendships, but they concluded that in these matters priests were probably no different from other American males. I would be inclined to add to that conclusion the comment that our data would suggest that whatever lack of capacity for intimate friendship is to be found among Catholic priests, it is more likely to be a result of childhood personality formation experiences than any result of seminary training or experience in the ministry. That one sleeps with a woman every night is no necessary guarantee that one has the capacity for intimate friendship. The capacity for friendship, all other things being equal, is probably formed early by the mother, father, child triad and by the way one handles the late adolescent crisis of identity. The seminary, the priesthood, and the Church have practically nothing to do with what goes on in the first experience, and have probably relatively little impact on the second. The seminary didn't provide much help in the resolution of the crises of intimacy and identity, and in the ideal order of things, one would expect that an institution committed to the Christian vision of things would have in fact facilitated maturational struggles. It didn't, but our data would indicate that it didn't hurt either. It may well be true that many priests have only vestigial capacities for intimacy. However, it is very likely that had they chosen other occupations and acquired wives and children along the way, their capacities for intimacy would not have been all that much improved, or improved at all.

2. We will note in a later chapter that only 10 per cent of the resignees want to return to doing those kinds of things that most priests do most of the time. The overwhelming

majority of resigned priests have no desire at all to go back to the active, full-time parochial or educational ministry, even if they could bring their wives along. This coincides with the finding in the present chapter that in fact the resignees did not get nearly as much satisfaction as active priests do (even the young ones) out of precisely that kind of behavior which is required of most priests most of the time. The cultic, ministerial, and educational functions of the priesthood provide considerable satisfactions to those who are in the priesthood, but resignees remember such activities as providing less satisfaction to them. On the other hand, the resignees are more likely to have enjoyed the social action dimensions of the priesthood than do those presently active in the ministry. While one cannot say that men left the priesthood because they did not like the work, one can say that dislike of the work does have some impact on loneliness, which in turn leads to an increase in the desire to marry, which in its turn leads to a propensity to resign.

3. One of the most interesting phenomena we observed in contemporary American Catholicism is the attempt, particularly of the younger generation of clergy and laity, to work out a new set of relationships with one another. The pre-Conciliar style of lay-clergy relationships emphasized a fixed, rigid protocol that was centuries old, and so sacred as to not to admit of violation save by the very brave. It would be a mistake, though, to think that there was no affection or even intimacy in such relationships. For all the wide-screen, soap-opera effect of the movie *Ryan's Daughter*, it presented, I think, an extraordinarily sympathetic portrait of the relationship between a west-of-Ireland parish priest and his people. The priest, splendidly played by Trevor Howard, was rough, crude, occasionally very autocratic, but at the same time gentle, sensitive, and extraordinarily affectionate toward his people. The relationship between this priest and Ryan's unfortunate daughter and her equally unfortunate husband was stylized in a very Irish and very pre-Conciliar fashion, yet it did not follow that it was

not an authentic and human relationship; on the contrary, it was a relationship in which there was a great deal of love, a love almost entirely implicit.[1] Had the style of that film relationship been replaced by the much more casual, informal relationships advocated in the American Church, it is unlikely that the love between Trevor Howard and his parishioners would have been strengthened; it might have made it impossible.

Nonetheless, we do not for weal or woe live in the west of Ireland during the First World War (with the IRA and MGM lurking on the beaches), and however much the styles of the past may have served the needs of the past, it is obvious that increasingly they do not serve the needs of the present. On balance, and all other things being equal (which they rarely are), the new, more flexible relationships emerging between clergy and lay people are probably an improvement over the old ones, but the important question is not whether the new is superior to the old. Can the new meet the needs of the present as well as if not better than the old met the needs of the past? I am inclined to think that the new will represent an improvement, but I do not believe that this will automatically be so. Sports shirts and first names (to say nothing of dirty jokes) do not necessarily improve the quality of human relationships. I suppose no one would claim that they did, but some behavior to be observed in clerical circles gives the impression that a few priests implicitly behave as though these short-cut symbols are an adequate substitute for the long, painful, frustrating, and discouraging process of developing a whole new style of relationships.

4. For some priests there is a very strong tendency to believe that they must try to "be like everyone else" and to be "accepted for who they are, not just because they are priests." Such attitudes, I think, are sociologically naïve, for of course one is not like everyone else by the very fact that one is a religious

---

[1] We Irish are not very good at making any kind of positive, warm human emotion explicit.

functionary. (To a lesser extent this would be true of an M.D., and especially a psychiatrist.) Furthermore, most contemporary American Catholics aren't very different from any other religious people in the course of history; they do not want their clergy to be just like everyone else. It is my impression that most of the laity, especially the young laity, want priests who are human beings with both human likability and human problems; but they also want human beings who have deep religious convictions and who see one of their principal purposes of life to be to proclaim both by word and deed these convictions. On the other hand, some priests are not convinced that religion is "relevant" any more; they think they can obtain acceptance as human beings either by being "nice guys" or social welfare agents or therapists or even radical social reformers. The laity I know do not object to these roles for a priest, but in addition they also want him to be a priest, by which I take it they mean him to be a man of God. I believe the need for religious faith and religious leadership is stronger in modern society than it has ever been before in human history. We thus have the rather paradoxical situation in which the laity may be looking for religious leaders more intensively than they ever have before while the clergy is more hesitant of playing the role of religious leaders than they ever have before. This contradiction may be soluble, though a solution will require the development of both the common vocabulary into a new, if much less stylized, set of role expectations. In the present situation the clergy are afraid to be too explicit in talking about religion and the laity are afraid to demand too explicitly that their priests talk about religion. The communication problem involved in this peculiar and hesitant dialogue can be overcome, but it will take time, perhaps more time than the present crisis in the Church will allow. In other words, it is possible that just as we will have to recover a sense of the importance of prayer, celibacy, and ecclesiastical structure, so it may well be into the next century before we recover a sense of the importance of the priesthood—

a sense which in the world of *Ryan's Daughter* was so much taken for granted as to be part of the environment.

5. The most frequently mentioned problem for priests is not celibacy but authority. Nevertheless, until the time of the present writing, the emphasis on reform in the Church seems to have been on the celibacy issue, not on the authority issue. There are two reasons for this: (1) the mass media, particularly as influenced by the liberal Catholic "opinion makers," has decided that celibacy is the principal problem, and many of the more militant clergy are responding more to the media than they are to the actual needs of their presumed constituencies. (2) While celibacy is a serious problem for only a small minority of priests, it is a very intense problem for that group, many of whom would like to marry and remain as priests—though probably not as priests in the full-time parochial or educational ministry. In other words, their own problem is more intense and more salient for them than are the problems of other priests, and therefore—and quite legitimately—they bring to an elaboration of an agenda of clerical militancy very strong personal feelings.

In a previous chapter I made clear my own conviction that power is a more important issue for the Catholic priesthood than sex, and that the sex problems will only be resolved when the power problems are. However, as we shall observe in a subsequent chapter, it is sex rather than power that leads people to resign from the priesthood, and if one is persuaded that the principal crisis facing the Church is the resignation of priests, then the celibacy issue is one that must be given high priority. If, on the other hand, one is concerned about the organizational effectiveness of the Church and the morale of the overwhelming majority of the clergy, the authority issue is more important than anything else. Obviously, in any practical program of reform, both problems must be addressed simultaneously.

6. It must be emphasized that even though almost three out of ten say that the way authority is exercised in the Church is

a great problem for them, only half that number think that relationships with their immediate superiors or pastors is a great problem for them. Authority, then, is a more general situation rather than the concrete circumstances in which one works. It is important to emphasize that most priests do not consider their personal situation to be intolerable because of the authority of the one who is the next rank up on the ecclesiastical ladder. Most priests do not live in circumstances of personal oppression. Whether the kinds of structural reform described in the previous chapter could eliminate the "authority problem" remains to be seen—and since the structural reforms are not likely to occur in the immediate future, we may have a long time to wait before we discover the effectiveness of such reforms. To the extent that the authority problem is a projection of one's own unresolved childhood conflicts, ecclesiastical reform will not eliminate the problems. By no means all citizens of our democratic society are free from "hangups" on democratically elected authority figures; on the other hand, to the extent that the authority problem responds to a situation in which priests find many of their leaders to be both unresponsive and irresponsible, to be men incapable of providing the context of faith, hope, and love to greatly facilitate their work in the priesthood, then the authority problem is not a projection, and institutional reform will lead to its diminution if not its elimination. Obviously, both projection and reality are blended in priests' perceptions of the authority problem. The data available to us do not permit us to say what the proportions of the blend are; however, in practice, it may not much matter. The Church has a long way to go down the road of institutional reform before it can begin to ask how much more reform would be merely a response to unresolved childhood anxieties.

7. The "loneliness" issue, which is not unrelated to the "getting through to people" issue, is a subtle and complicated one. It cannot be analyzed either with our data or, indeed, with the technology of survey research, unfortunately. The recent study

by the Gallup organization of clergymen of all three major denominations shows that frustrations in getting through to people are by no means limited to Catholic priests. It is perhaps part of the nature of the profession—only in psychiatry and, possibly, neurosurgery is the proportion of failures so high. The priest is dealing with the supermundane, the transcendent, and however much man needs them, he frequently finds these realities difficult, distracting, and bothersome. Ideally, it seems, we hedge our bets, and throw ourselves with vigor into the pleasures, preoccupations, cares, and anxieties of this world while at the same time maintaining some kind of moderately cordial relationships with whatever realities may exist beyond this world. We deem it appropriate to give anxious concern to what we should eat, drink, and put on, while at the same time assuring the Ground of Being, or whatever else It or He may be, that we do take seriously His power and injunctions. The clergyman is in some fashion the local representative of the Ground of Being and he must be dealt with, placated, kept reasonably happy, but not taken either too seriously or too literally. We are ready to acknowledge, if pushed to it, that this puts him in a fairly difficult situation, but then, he knew what he was getting into. Who knows? Maybe he felt a strong inner need to experience frustration. Why else become a cleric in the first place?

There is probably nothing that can be done in the way of institutional reform of the Church that will eliminate or even notably reduce frustration, discouragement, and disappointment in the priests' dealing with the people. The best that can be expected is that a priest would have enough sufficient sophistication and emotional maturity to understand that there is going to be only relatively moderate payoff for all his effort. Given the nature of the human condition, this is all he can reasonably expect. Priests cannot avoid frustration in their lives and work; they must learn to accept it and deal with it.

8. Loneliness is another problem. No man can operate effec-

tively or even survive very long as a human being if he is lonely, especially if loneliness is an abiding problem for him. Loneliness is obviously related to celibacy; indeed, it has a simple correlation coefficient of .51 with the desire to marry, which is another way of saying that a very high proportion of those priests who want to marry are to be found in that approximately one sixth of the clergy who report that loneliness is a serious problem for them. We are much less successful at explaining why some priests fall into that one sixth and most others do not. The lonely ones tend to be younger, have more modern values, and are apt to find less satisfaction in their work; however, they score no lower than the nonlonely on the scale measuring self-actualization. One cannot therefore argue either that the lonely priests are the strong ones brave enough to break with an outmoded authoritarian Church or that they are the weak ones who can no longer take the strain of a committed life. Our data suggest that neither strength or weakness is a predictor of loneliness, at least in so far as the POI scale measures these personality dimensions. Whether loneliness can be resolved by marriage is an open question. We will see later that the answer to this question is at best ambiguous. However, if one is a celibate, he has the possibility of blaming his unmarried state for his feelings of loneliness. If one is lonely and married, celibacy obviously cannot be blamed. Thus, even if celibacy is not the cause of loneliness (and I do not assert that: I only advance it as a hypothetical condition), it is certainly reasonable for a lonely person to think celibacy does cause loneliness and to expect that marriage would help solve the problem.

There is not much talk of loneliness among priests, and our data suggest that not all that many priests think that loneliness is a problem for them, but there are more who think it is a great problem than talk about it. Most of us are quite incapable of guessing whether a colleague feels lonely or not, or at least before his loneliness drives him out of the priesthood.

Whether loneliness has increased in the last decade is problematic. It could be argued on the one hand that the greater freedom of the present Church simply makes it more feasible for men to leave the priesthood in order to escape from their loneliness. It also can be argued that the collapse of the old rigid structures and the resulting chaos and confusion have actually increased for many priests the amount of loneliness in their lives. My own hunch is that while there is an element of truth in both explanations, the former is more persuasive than the latter. The dramatic changes of the past decade have not so much caused an increase in loneliness as to permit the loneliness already there to come to the surface.

RECOMMENDATIONS

1. It must be recognized that the job of a clergyman, even if he is married, but especially if he is celibate, is a discouraging and frustrating one. The clergy, if they are to be successful, need powerful emotional support from their colleagues, their leaders, and from the people. In American Catholicism, this fact has not been faced, and it is generally assumed by Church leadership, by Catholic people, and by the priests themselves that the priest is something of an iron man who can cope with the aloneness of his life, the frustrations of his work, the difficulties and confusions of his own personal growth without any emotional support, much less affection, from anyone. Celibacy is not going to survive in either an obligatory or optional form until ways are found both in theory and practice to provide emotional support and response in the life of a celibate. Obviously, this response and support have existed in the past, but they have existed largely in spite of the theory and not because of it. It is therefore necessary to elaborate a theory of emotional support for the clergy and then to implement it in a wide variety of practical measures, the most important of which would be strong colleague-support groups among priests. Furthermore, those laity who become involved in close cooperation with

priests ("priest fans," as one of my former pastors used to sneeringly call them) should realize that priests are not only human beings, but human beings who are committed to discouraging and frustrating work and who may not have available the emotional resources that marriage provides for some (though by no means all) married people. To work out relationships of friendship and support will take time, taste, and patience. Most priests can do without those kinds of laity who want to mother them; a priest does not need a mother—though some priests who marry may be looking for one. A priest needs an adult friend with whom he can share hopes, aspirations, problems, and discouragements. He needs these friends not because he is some sort of pitiable and pathetic creature who wants to be loved, but because all human beings need love, especially those whose principal work is with other human beings.

2. It is discouraging to see that for many priests the discovery of the need for friendship and emotional support leads to juvenile and adolescent behavior—"crushes," weird therapy groups, infatuations, phony honesty, and emotional exhibitionism. Such aberrations are an inevitable cost of the shift in ideology from the conviction that priests really ought not to have personal friends who are not priests (and ought even to be wary of "particular" friendships with other priests) to an ideology that includes priests in the human condition that people develop emotionally through relationships. Ecclesiastical leadership and the various kinds of priest organizations ought to encourage and support in whatever way they can the development of stronger support mechanisms in the lives of priests. Whether a priest is any less capable than anyone else of intimate friendship (and I doubt that he is) is less relevant than the question of how a priest can enrich his capacity for intimacy. The leader of a religious community in a personalist age will not be very effective unless he is capable of providing strong emotional support for his people, and he won't be able to provide that support unless he experiences it in his own life. To experience it in one's

own life means that the support is there and that one knows how to respond to it when it is offered. This matter is of utmost importance, no matter how the celibacy issue is resolved. Even if one is not convinced as I am that loneliness is probably independent of whether one is married or not, priests need the strength and support that intimate relationships provide.

3. While the fairly high level of satisfaction with colleague relationships is encouraging and perhaps surprising, there is still probably a need for priests to develop more sophisticated skills in collaborating closely with each other and with lay people. While we did not hope to discover how many clerical "lone wolves" there were, one certainly has the strong impression that such individualists are fairly numerous. If they are young, they may speak of "doing their own thing," if older, they may speak of "making their own decisions." In either case, they find it very difficult to yoke themselves to the restraints of close collaboration with others. The priesthood may have no greater share of such individualists than other professions, and surely their scores on the POI scale would not sustain the assertion that large numbers of priests are "hyperindependent." Nevertheless, the priesthood is certainly the kind of profession in which the close collaboration of men with different skills, talents, insights, and personal qualities would be extremely important. Teamwork requires trust, and while there may be no less trust among priests than among other groups in the population, a fairly convincing argument can be made that there is a greater need for trust among priests. It is hard to acquire skills of cooperation when one has not learned in infancy, childhood, and adolescence how to trust others; but because it is difficult does not mean it is impossible. Ecclesiastical leadership and priest associations, therefore, should do all they can to make available to priests experiences in which they can improve their skills at cooperation.

I hardly need add that such experiences should be voluntary and supervised by professionally trained practitioners. No claims should be made for marvelous and rapid transformation of the personality, and in such experiences the psychodynamics should be carefully explained. Participants should be screened beforehand to make sure that they will not be harmed by the experience. The widespread misuse of sensitivity training and other forms of group dynamics ought not blind us to the important positive contributions they can make. Because their contributions may be limited does not mean they are worthless; because some naïve enthusiasts claim foolish things for sensitivity training does not mean that it cannot in some circumstances be moderately helpful.

One ecclesiastical administrator, who is also a trained psychologist, remarked to me in a moment of discouragement, "We have to write off everybody over thirty-five." I can understand his discouragement, but however correct his analysis may be as a prediction of what will happen, the Church can ill afford to adopt it as policy. On the contrary, it seems to me that the policy to which the Church can commit itself on the subject of the maturation of the clergy is enunciated in the famous words of the psychologist Nevitt Stanford, "We are never too old to grow."

IO

THE MORALE OF THE CLERGY

FINDINGS

In the previous chapter, we observed that the work of the priest was discouraging and frustrating. Here, we will report that the psychological well-being of priests is on the average higher than that of typical college-educated married males in the same age categories. Despite the discouragement and loneliness, then, the morale of priests is in fact better than the morale of typical American males.

The measures of psychological well-being were developed by Professor Norman Bradburn, former director of the National Opinion Research Center. Bradburn's model of psychological well-being is a "hydraulic" one; that is to say, he sees happiness as a favorable balance of payments between positive and negative feelings. A person can be "happy" with many negative emotions so long as the positive emotions are more powerful and outweigh the negative ones. Similarly, he can have a favorable balance of payments if his positive affect is low but not quite so low as the negative. In operationalizing his model, Bradburn has developed measures of both positive and negative affect in a balance scale which results from a person's negative affect being subtracted from his positive affect.

1. As we see in the accompanying table, there is no difference in positive affect between priests and college-educated married men of the same age categories except among those over fifty-five, and in this instance, given the negative correlation Bradburn and his colleagues have found between age and positive affect and the small number of respondents among the married males, the comparison is dubious.

2. The real difference between priests and married men is in negative affect. At each of the age levels, priests report less negative affect than do married males, and very considerably less negative affect than do unmarried lay males. This led Professor Bradburn to comment, not altogether facetiously, "If you're not married, it helps to be a priest."

3. On the affect balance scale, which in Bradburn's model drafts psychological well-being or happiness, the scores of priests are consistently higher and indeed substantially higher than those of college-educated married men in the same age groups.

4. As we can see from the second accompanying table, negative affect increases and positive affect declines until a decision is made to resign from the priesthood. Those who are uncertain or will probably resign have an affect score which only varies slightly on the favorable side. However, once the decision to resign is made, psychological well-being begins to increase and continues to climb for the first three years after resignation when it begins to decline, largely through an increase in negative affect. Even for those who resigned five years before the data were collected, the affect balance score is no lower than those of priests who were definitely committed to leaving the priesthood. Whether the psychological well-being of the resignees will continue to decline or not remains to be seen. However, given the declining levels of satisfaction in their marriages, which we will report in a subsequent chapter, there is some reason to expect a further decline in psychological well-being.

TABLE 1   AFFECT SCALE SCORES OF PRIESTS
AND COLLEGE-EDUCATED MALES, BY AGE
(Mean Scores)

Age	Active Priests	College-educated males[a] (non-priests)	
		Married	Unmarried
	Positive affect scale		
26–35	3.7 (1094)	3.7 (58)	
36–45	3.4 (1526)	3.5 (41)	
46–55	3.2 (1155)	3.2 (32)	
Over 55	2.7 (1313)	3.2 (10)	
Total	3.4 (5088)	3.5 (141)	3.2[b] (20)
	Negative affect scale		
26–35	1.9 (1094)	2.6 (58)	
36–45	1.5 (1526)	2.2 (41)	
46–55	1.1 (1155)	1.3 (32)	
Over 55	.7 (1313)	1.9 (10)	
Total	1.0 (5088)	2.2 (141)	2.8[b] (20)
	Affect balance scale		
26–35	1.8 (1094)	1.1 (58)	
36–45	2.0 (1526)	1.3 (41)	
46–55	2.2 (1155)	1.0 (32)	
Over 55	2.0 (1313)	.3 (10)	
Total	2.4 (5088)	1.3 (141)	.4[b] (20)

[a] Data from NORC Happiness Study, 1963.
[b] Not enough cases for breakdown by age.

TABLE 2   AFFECT SCALE SCORES OF ACTIVE PRIESTS
AND RESIGNEES
(Mean Scores)

Item	Positive Affect Scale	Negative Affect Scale	Affect Balance Scale	N
Active priests (by future plans in priesthood):				
Definitely will not leave	3.2	.9	2.3	2,933
Probably will not leave	3.4	1.6	1.8	1,553
Uncertain	3.0	2.3	.7	447
Probably will leave	2.8	2.2	.6	97
Definitely decided to leave	3.4	2.1	1.3	59
Resigned priests (by year of resignation):				
1970	4.1	1.7	2.4	24
1969	4.2	1.3	2.9	301
1968	4.2	1.2	3.0	228
1967	4.2	1.4	2.8	123
1966	4.0	1.5	2.5	47
1964–65	4.0	1.7	2.3	16

SPECULATIONS

1. I think that most of us were surprised by the findings reported in the previous section. Given the stresses and strains in both the priestly life and the present crisis in the Church, the best that we expected was that the psychological well-being of priests was no worse than comparable American males. If anything, one would have expected priests to score better on the positive affect scale. If priests were to do better than other Americans, one would have thought that they would have more positive affect rather than less negative affect than the compari-

son groups. An argument could have been made that the priest-hood as a way of life held more payoff and more frustration; in fact, the finding was that the emotional payoffs for priests seemed to be about the same as that for married college-edu-cated males, and their negative experiences to be rather less than that of college-educated males.[1]

There is, then, apparently no less positive payoff in the life of a priest than in the life of a typical American male, and considerably less frustration. Why this should be the case is not immediately clear. One would very much like to have compara-ble data on Protestant ministers to see if their scores on the negative affect measure are lower than the scores of their lay counterparts. Does the data reported in the previous section contradict my assertion of the last chapter that the work of the priest is more discouraging than the work of most people, or might it be that there are fewer frustrations and problems in other areas of life for a priest despite the frustrations of his work? Could it be that the absence of financial concerns and the responsibilities of raising a family explain the rather low nega-tive affect of priests? If this, indeed, is the explanation, then we might suggest that there is something to be said for poverty and chastity, especially since marriage and family do not give the married males in the comparison groups any advantage over priests in positive affect.

2. There is something "wrong" about the tables presented at the beginning of the chapter. "Everyone knows" that priests should have less emotional payoff than married men, and "every-one knows" that they should have more frustrations, but in fact the finding persists: Priests have no less emotional payoff and substantially less frustrations. If what "everyone knows" turns out to be wrong, then it follows that the model that produced

[1] Lest some suspicious reader think that we are hiding something by dealing only with college-educated men, let me emphasize that psychologi-cal well-being correlated positively with college attendance. If the compari-son was between priests and all American males, priests would look even better.

that finding ought to be re-examined. If a decade and a half ago, the data in this chapter had been presented, there might have been much less surprise, because at that time the image of the priest was of a dedicated, committed man, who had chosen the celibate priesthood because he expected to find greater happiness in the service of God in this life. While he would miss the joys of marriage and family, there would be compensations in the sense of dedication to the work of God. Furthermore, the single-minded nature of his dedication would eliminate from his life many of the distractions, cares, and worries experienced by many other men. There would be less reason for him to give anxious heed to what he should eat, or drink, or put on. This model has seemed less persuasive in recent years because of the number of men who have left the priesthood, because of the books and articles some of them have written, because of the sympathy for the poor, suffering, frustrated priest presented by some liberal Catholic journalists. According to the new model, the priest is a man who was tricked into commitments he really never understood; he is lonely, frustrated, and unhappy in his work; he desperately misses the rewards of sex and family life, and he wants to break free from the rigid constraints under which he has been forced to live in order that he might have a chance to become fully a man. This model has been repeated so persistently that I think it was taken for granted by most non-Catholic Americans who spend any time reading the national journals. It is also taken seriously by large numbers of Catholic lay people, and perhaps even by many priests. Our data suggest —and very strongly—that the newer model has rather little validity; the older model is still a remarkably accurate description of the state of the priesthood.

3. Not all priests are happy, of course, and one can see from Table 2 that there is a strong relationship between unhappiness and propensity to leave the priesthood. In other words, low morale among the clergy is confined to that group which is either probably going to leave the priesthood or uncertain about

whether it will leave or stay, a group which includes somewhere between 10 and 15 per cent of the priests. For this group, the morale problem is very serious indeed; but this group is not typical of the American priesthood. The newer model may well apply to them; it does not apply to the other 85 per cent of the clergy.

The most powerful predictor of negative affect available to us is, as one might well surmise, loneliness. The correlation between negative affect and loneliness is .45. Indeed, the relationship between the two is so close that in the causal model we will explain in the next chapter, we use loneliness instead of negative affect as the variable representing the morale problem. However, most of the causes of negative affect are apparently filtered through either loneliness or lack of satisfaction with work (—.3). To the extent that we can explain the morale problem (and we can explain about 30 per cent of the variants on the negative affect scale, a not unimpressive performance), we can say that it is the result of high levels of loneliness and low levels of work satisfaction. But most priests are not lonely, and most priests are reasonably satisfied with their work; hence most priests score low on the negative affect scale and consequently score high on the balance scale. Therefore, we may tentatively conclude that priests' morale is high in part because most priests are reasonably satisfied with their work and do not experience loneliness as a great problem. This explanation runs against much of the current conventional wisdom, but until more sophisticated studies are done on the morale of the clergy, I think the conventional wisdom must be seriously doubted.

4. One of the more interesting things that might have been observed in the first table of this chapter was that both negative and positive affect correlate with youthfulness. Young priests have higher scores on both scales with the net result that on the balance scale, they are not much different from the older clergy. (The correlation between age and positive affect is —32; between age and negative affect, it is —33; and between age and

affect balance, it is .01.) Thus, to the extent that Bradburn's measures of psychological well-being tap the very amorphous thing we call morale, it can be asserted that the morale of the younger clergy is neither better nor worse than that of the older clergy. There may very well be different components of the favorable balance of payments between positive and negative affect for young priests than the mix of components that go into the psychological well-being of older priests; however, the net result is the same. Younger priests are indeed more likely to think of resigning from the priesthood, but not because their psychological well-being is any worse than that of older priests. The myth of the morale crisis, then, among the young clergy is in all likelihood false. What is available to the younger clergy is a greater opportunity for marriage. It is easier for a younger priest than for an older priest to persuade himself that his loneliness and his frustrations can be attributed to the celibate state, and they will be eliminated when he finds himself a wife. I am not saying that such an argument is not true in some, or many, or even most cases; I am simply saying that it is an argument that is easier to make when you are young.

5. It would be easy to take the findings of this chapter out of context to argue that there are no real problems facing the American priesthood because psychological well-being of priests is not only reasonably high, it is higher than that of comparable married men. However, reality is more complex than that. Even if the morale of priests is high, there is still a large number of resignations from the priesthood in the last five years. There is no reason to think that the resignation rate will decline in the immediate future, and though the Gallup study of the clergy of three main denominations showed that Protestant and Jewish clergy were still more likely to think seriously of resigning than the Catholic clerics, the resignation problem is still a new one for the priesthood. If it does not represent a morale crisis for the priesthood as a whole, it does represent a morale crisis for a moderate-sized segment of the priesthood, a segment which did

not have this problem before. Furthermore, even though morale remains high despite the authority problem we discussed earlier, the proper conclusion would be not that nothing needs to be done about authority, but that the personal, psychological well-being of most priests can survive despite authority problems. The structure of the Church then should be reformed not to make priests feel better but to enable them to do their work more effectively. Finally, one could also make a case that given their religious commitments and the faith about the nature and destiny of the universe, the positive affect of priests should not only be comparable with that of other American males, it should be much higher. That priests are somewhat happier than other men is good news, but they should be much happier than other men if they really believe the Good News.

RECOMMENDATIONS

1. It is hard to make recommendations on the subject of the psychological well-being of priests, since in general it turns out to be rather impressive. One must insist, however, that the psychological well-being of the majority does not mean that there are not serious morale problems for certain segments of the clergy, morale problems closely related to loneliness and to the propensity to resign from the priesthood. If ecclesiastical leadership wishes to do anything to decrease the resignation rate—and sometimes I am not persuaded that it does—then it must be seriously concerned about the fact that somewhere between one sixth and one seventh of the priesthood is lonely, dissatisfied, and unhappy. Whether the low morale of this group will infect the other approximately 85 per cent of the clergy is something that only the future can tell, but it would be unwise of anyone to assume that any such contagion is impossible; too many unexpected things have happened in the priesthood in the last decade to rule out anything as impossible.

2. On the other hand, the new model of the conventional

wisdom of the priest as a lonely, frustrated, unhappy man ought to be given a decent burial; indeed, priests themselves should stop taking it seriously. That there are lonely, unhappy, frustrated men in the priesthood is true, but that the typical priest is lonely, unhappy, and frustrated is not true, and we should not let anyone try to persuade us that it is. The problem is, of course, that we see men leaving the priesthood because their unhappiness, and we wonder whether that unhappiness pervades the entire priesthood. Most of us do not feel all that unhappy ourselves, but we begin to wonder whether we ought to be. The data collected in our study suggest that at least as far as numbers go, the norm for the priest is a level of psychological well-being higher than that of his married counterpart.

II

WHY THEY LEAVE

THE CAUSAL MODEL

In this chapter I shall abandon the practice of keeping the sociological apparatus at a minimum. The causal model that the NORC team developed to explain why people are inclined to leave the priesthood is not difficult for the nonprofessional reader to understand. While a whole book of such models might be overpowering, I think one chapter on such a model will prove to the lay (i.e., nonsociologist, in this context) reader to be extremely helpful.

The goal of any social research endeavor is explanation. The researcher is not merely interested in what is happening but in why it is happening. Hence, in the final analysis he is interested in "causal" explanation. It is not enough to know that variable A is related to variable B; one does all in one's power to establish that A causes B. A causal connection is rather easy to establish under some circumstances. If one knows, for example, that while in college a young man had planned to enter medical school and one discovers a statistical relationship between these plans and his present attendance at medical school, one can say that his plans while in college were in part a cause of his present attendance, although obviously they were not the only or a completely effective cause.

It may be that a number of readers will not wish to pursue the detailed analytic reasoning presented in this chapter. Therefore, we will present the fundamental findings of the chapter before we go into the analysis. The reader who wishes to skip the analysis will find "Speculations" on page 184.

FINDINGS

1. There is no evidence to suggest that on the national level resignation rates of priests are likely to decline in the foreseeable future.

2. If only that 3 per cent who said they were probably or definitely going to leave do in fact resign in the near future, there will be almost two thousand more resignations. If substantial numbers of those who are uncertain or who say they probably will not leave should in fact decide to resign, the numbers could be very much higher.

3. A substantial number of American priests have been forced to rethink their own positions in the priesthood because of the rising resignation rate.

4. The most frequently mentioned reason for leaving the priesthood is the desire to marry. However, various aspects of frustration in priestly work in *combination* are mentioned even more frequently.

5. The principal reasons for staying in the priesthood as given by our respondents are a sense of vocation and happiness in the work. Younger priests also mention a desire to be a witness to Christ and to reform the structures of the Church.

6. When we turn from given reasons for resignations to sophisticated analytic techniques, we discover that a desire to marry is the strongest predictor of plans to leave the priesthood, in part because a desire to marry acts as a "channel" for prior causes of resignation.

7. The principal reason for the desire to marry is loneliness.

8. And the factors which influence loneliness are youthfulness, inner-directed personality, more modern values, a tense

family background, a lower level of religious experience, and a lower level of work satisfaction.

The complexity of social reality is such that it is extremely difficult to determine the direction of a causal flow between two variables when a relationship has been demonstrated between them. For example, we shall point out in this chapter that there is a negative relationship between holding certain "modern" values about the nature of the Church and future plans to stay in the priesthood. We assume that the values are logically prior to the plans, though we cannot exclude the possibility that someone's values are in part the result of his future plans rather than the cause; nor can we rule out the chance that there is some "feedback" effect, that values and plans mutually affect each other.

What the researcher does is to establish certain "models" as tools for analyzing reality. These models are statements of causal relationships based on a number of specified assumptions about the flow of causality among the variables he is considering. The assumptions are not arbitrary but are based on what the researcher thinks are the most solid theoretical or chronological reasons. (One's values, for example, cannot be assumed to have caused one's parents' education.) The model is an "as if" device. The researcher analyzes his variables "as if" the causal flow in reality is the way he has specified it in his model. The model can then be used as a tool for examining reality, but it does not claim to be an exact duplicate of reality. Another researcher might make a different set of assumptions and examine reality in a different fashion. What is important is that a researcher specify his assumptions before the data become available, and that he make these specifications and the reasons for them explicit. A refusal to specify a causal model leaves both the researcher and his audience in a morass of correlations that cannot be arranged in any meaningful fashion. Once a model has been stated, the relationships are arranged in one meaningful fashion, though it may not be necessarily the only possible fashion.

In Figure 1 we present graphically the model on which the analysis in this chapter is based. The causal flow is from left to right. Each variable is assumed to have a possible direct and indirect causal relationship with each variable to its right. For example, age is assumed to have a possible causal influence on personality, religious experience, values, work problems, morale, the desire to marry, and future plans with regard to the priesthood. This influence may be direct or it may flow through any variable that intervenes between age and a later variable. Thus, age may have a direct influence on work problems as well as indirect influences through personality, religious experience, and values. Our work of analysis will be to put lines between these boxes and to put numbers on the lines to determine the actual existence of and the strength of causal relationships among the nine variables in the model.

Let us make clear our assumptions:

1. We do not postulate a causal connection between age and family tension because there is no logical or chronological reason for doing so. They thus appear at the same level of the model.

2. We assume on the basis of general social science theory that personality is the result of background demographic and social psychological variables such as age and family tension.

3. We assume that religious experience—sense of contact with the Deity—is influenced by family background and in its turn is part of the psycho-religious equipment that one brings to the ministry.

4. We assume that religious values are shaped by background, personality, and experience of the divine, and that they in turn shape the reaction to one's work in the ministry.

5. We assume that the problems, frustrations, and difficulties (of the satisfactions, joys, and fulfillments) in one's work are shaped by an interaction of background, personality, religious experience, and values.

6. We view morale, or psychological well-being, as being the result of the reaction to one's work experience as interpreted in

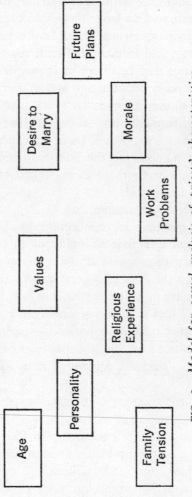

FIG. 1 *Model for casual analysis of priests' characteristics.*

the light of background, personality, religious experience, and values, and as a possible cause of the desire to marry, and of the decision to resign from the priesthood (or to stay in the priesthood).

7. We have placed the desire to marry in a rather late position in our model for three reasons. First of all, social science theory would lead us to predict that low satisfaction in priestly work would lead to a desire to marry as a compensation for the lack of "payoff" in the work, while a high level of payoff in terms of the satisfaction and fulfillments of the work might lead to a decline in the difficulties with celibacy. Secondly, an inspection of the percentages of those wishing to marry leads us to believe on empirical grounds that only a relatively small proportion of the clergy would in fact marry if they could. Finally, in terms of analytic strategy our model enables us to measure the increment to the amount of dissatisfaction priests experience that can be attributed only to the desire to marry. Or, to put the matter somewhat differently, our strategy makes it possible to estimate the contribution of celibacy to resignation among the clergy, *net of all other sources of dissatisfaction.*

Model building is not a completely rational business. Insight, instinct, and intuition go into it; and the statement of assumptions is usually an exercise in making explicit intuitive "feelings" about the shape of reality.[1] The ultimate test of a model is how useful it is for examining and understanding reality. We think that the model used in this chapter will prove to have some utility. Other researchers may devise other models, and NORC has traditionally stood ready to make its data available for the use of other model builders.

The model presented in Figure 1 is a version of one that was stated before inspection of the data began. The logic of our assumptions was explicit from the early stages of the project.

---

[1] We share the feelings of such philosophers of science as Michael Polanyi and Thomas Kuhn that the quasi-artistic insight is at the core of scientific activity.

However, this figure is much simpler than earlier versions because many variables were dropped from the model when we found that they did not play an important role. Thus, we had first assumed that variables such as parental education, age at entry of the seminary, amount of postseminary education, being a member of a religious order, and size of one's diocese or religious order would correlate with the variables presently in the model. However, no important correlations (in excess of .2) emerged between these variables and those presently in the model. Occasionally a variable would correlate with one element of the model but with no other element, and it was dropped. Thus, we found a relationship between family religious devotion and recollection of family tension, but religious devotion did not correlate with any of the other variables in the model, and we dropped it from further analysis.

Furthermore, a number of different variables could be put in the specific boxes in Figure 1. There are several different indicators of values, of work problems, and of morale. The final decision as to which ones to use depended on which displayed the strongest correlations with the variables to the right of the box about which the decision had to be made.

Only one variable was added to the model in the course of the analysis—the reports of respondents on whether loneliness was a serious problem for them in the priesthood. This variable was added because the desire to marry turned out to play such an important part in the model, and we hypothesized (correctly, as it turned out) that loneliness would strongly correlate with the desire to marry. That loneliness was not put into the model before inspection of the data was simply a mistake. It should have been but was not—a phenomenon that is as common in social research as in any other human enterprise.

The decisions about which variables to drop from the original, far more elaborate model and which indicators to use in the specific boxes were based on inspection of several large correlation matrices. The inspection of these matrices and the determination of which variables went into them took place in light of the expectations and assumptions we have already stated. We shall not burden the reader of this chapter with the many pages of numbers necessary to duplicate these matrices; however, copies of them are on file at NORC should any reader wish to examine them.

The technique we will use to analyze the relationship among the various factors in our causal model is called path analysis. It makes use of multiple regression statistics. The typical path diagram or multiple regression table may look overwhelming to the lay reader. In fact, with a bit of patience, the reader may discover that it is an easy way to conceptualize about social reality. Let us explain by way of example.

Figure 2 illustrates the kind of analysis that will be attempted. Let us assume a population of students that is ordered on three different scales—their age, the number of years of education they have had, and their scores on the Graduate Record Examination. Let us assume further that on their ages they may score anywhere from 1 to 25; on their education, anywhere from 1 to 16 years; and on their GRE scores, anywhere from 0 to 100. The correlation coefficient is the measure of the extent to which there is a relationship between one's position on one of these scales and his position on another scale. Thus, the relationship (r) of .32 between age and GRE score in Table 1 is a description of the extent of the relationship of where one is on the age scale and where one is on the GRE score scale. Since age is obviously something that is prior to taking the exam, it can be assumed that the position on the age scale is causally connected to one's exam score. In other words, the older you are, the more likely you are to get a good score. Moving to the column, r^2, which is simply r multiplied by itself, is the amount of variance on one scale that can be explained by variance on another scale. The r^2 between age and GRE score is .10, which means that about 10 per cent of the variance on the GRE score scale can be explained by age. Age "causes" 10 per cent of the differences among the

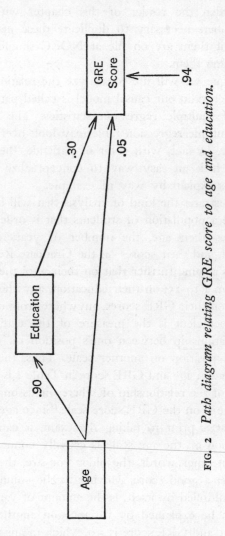

FIG. 2 Path diagram relating GRE score to age and education.

young people in their GRE score. But we also note from Table 1 that education relates to GRE score with a correlation of .30, so one's position on the education scale bears some relationship to one's performance in the exam. If age and education were completely independent of one another, their combined influence would give an R of .43 and an explanation of about 19 per cent of the variance on the exam score, but a moment's consideration makes it clear that there is a strong relationship between age and education, and therefore a substantial part of their causal influence on exam scores would overlap.

The statistic R is a measure of their joint influence on GRE score, and the statistic R^2 is the measure of the explanatory power of the two variables combined. We see from Table 1 that the R of age and education together (presented in the education row of the table) is .35, and that the R^2 is .12. The overlap between age and education is therefore quite considerable be-

TABLE 1   CORRELATIONS OF GRADUATE RECORD EXAMINATION SCORE WITH AGE AND EDUCATION

Variable	r	r^2	R	R^2	R^2 Change
Age	.32	.10	.32	.10	.10
Education	.30	.09	.35	.12	.02

cause when one adds education to the model, the R goes up by only 3 points and the R^2 by only 2 points. The final column of the table, R^2 change, shows the increase in the explanatory power of the model by adding education to the causal system containing age and GRE score.

One might assume from looking at the table, then, that age was the principal "cause" of a high score on the GRE, since our addition of education to the model only improves its explanatory power by 2 percentage points. However, another moment's consideration will reveal that this would be a false conclusion. In all likelihood, we would assume that what happens is that age is correlated with education and education, in turn, is correlated with one's position on the GRE score scale. Age, then, "causes" the number of years that the young person has attended school, and this in turn "causes" his position on the GRE measure. The flow chart in Figure 2 illustrates this relationship.[2]

There is a .90 correlation between age and education, a .30 correlation between education and GRE score, and a .05 relationship between age and GRE score with education taken into account. In other words, most of the influence of age flows through education to GRE score while a rather small proportion of the influence of age is direct. Older students get better scores mostly because they have had more schooling. The line linking age and GRE score is called the "direct path" between age and exam score, and the lines between age and education and between education and GRE score can be multiplied to produce the "indirect path" of age's influence on exam score. The measure of the indirect path is the product of the two path coefficients, or $.9 \times .3 = .27$. Thus, of the r of .32 between age and GRE score, .27 is indirect and .05 is direct.

The advantage of the diagram in Figure 2 is that it enables us to consider simultaneously the direct and indirect paths by which a prior variable influences a subsequent variable. In this particular instance, for example, we note that even though the addition of education to our model only improves our explanatory power by two percentage points, education is nevertheless the principal channel by which age exercises its influence on GRE score. A small R^2 change, therefore, does not indicate that the variable which causes this rather small addition to the explanatory power of the model is unimportant.

It will be noted that there is a third arrow pointing into GRE

[2] It should be observed, incidentally, that the model illustrated in Figure 2 is completely mythical and does not represent any actual data on the relationship between age, education, and GRE scores.

score with a .94 at its base. This third arrow is called the "residual path." The square of the residual path coefficient indicates the amount of variance in GRE score not explained by the model. Thus, .94 squared is .88. Twelve per cent of the variance in GRE score is explained by age and education, and 88 per cent of the variance remains unexplained by the model. It can be said, therefore, that age and education do in fact play some causal role in a young person's performance on the GRE, but even when their full causal impact is taken into account, 88 per cent of the variance in the position of students on the score scale remains to be explained.

Social science does not expect to be able to explain 100 per cent of the variance. Such determinism of human attitudes and behavior can scarcely be expected to exist in reality, however much it may have been honored in philosophical textbooks in the past. The amount of explained variance that satisfies the researcher depends upon the nature of the analysis in which he is engaged. However, the fact that we are able to explain as much as one half of the variance in future plans in the priesthood with a very complex causal model would be, we suspect, considered quite creditable by most of our sociological colleagues.

Finally, all path coefficients under .15 are dropped from the model in order that the strongest causal links may be the ones to receive principal emphasis.

The accompanying Table 2 shows that 3 per cent of the American priests are either probably or definitely going to leave the priesthood, and 10 per cent of the diocesan pirests and 7 per cent of the religious priests are uncertain as to whether they will stay or leave the priesthood. Our causal model is designed to determine where on this five-point scale a respondent will place himself.

Figure 3 represents the causal model around which the entire NORC research was analyzed. The first point to be made is that the —.17 correlation between family tension and age, represented by the vertical line at the left of the path diagram,

TABLE 2   FUTURE PLANS IN THE PRIESTHOOD,
BY CLERICAL STATUS
(Per Cent)

Future Plans in the Priesthood	Diocesan		Religious	
	Bishops	Active Priests	Major Superiors	Active Priests
Definitely will not leave	99	55	77	62
Probably will not leave	1	32	21	28
Uncertain	0	10	2	7
Probaby will leave	0	2	0	2
Definitely decided to leave	0	1	0	1
Total	100	100	100	100

means that these two variables are related to one another, but that we are unable to make a causal assumption about which might be prior to the other.

The second point to be emphasized is that the coefficients at the bottom and the top of the page, with arrows pointing in to the various boxes, are the residual coefficients. If one squares a residual coefficient and subtracts from 100, one has the amount of variance that is explained on the given scale to which the arrow points. For example, the residual coefficient on loneliness is .87; its square is .75; subtracting this from 100 tells us that 25 per cent of the variance on loneliness is explained. Similarly, 37 per cent of the variant of the desire to marry is explained, and 52 per cent of the variant on the future plan scale is explained. Given the fact that one is dealing necessarily with crude and imprecise measures, such explanatory power of a causal model is easily sufficient to make most social scientists dance up and down with happiness.

We may now inspect the model itself. It becomes obvious immediately that there are two causal systems at work which

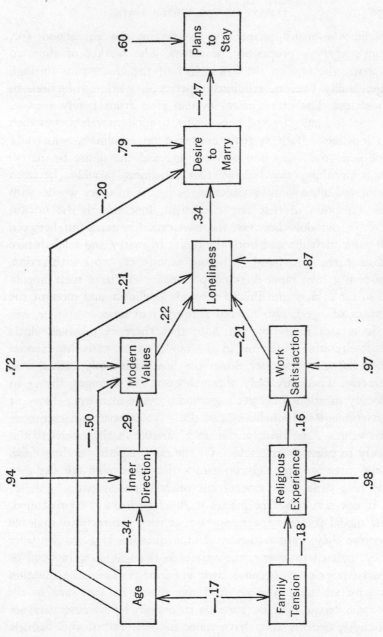

FIG. 3 Causal model for NORC research.

influence a man's propensity to stay in the priesthood (or, conversely, his propensity to leave). The weaker of the two systems, the one on the lower half of the chart, runs through age, family tension, religious experience, work satisfaction, to loneliness. The other causal system runs from family tension, to age, to inner-directed personality, to modern values, and then to loneliness. Both systems converge on loneliness, with only one path—the —.20 line between age and the desire to marry, short-circuiting the linkage that loneliness provides between prior and subsequent variables in the model. In other words, with the exception of that one coefficient, loneliness is the critical linkage, not only between the two causal systems but between all prior variables and both the desire to marry and one's future plans in the priesthood. Religious experience, work satisfaction, modern values, inner-directed personality—all have their impact in so far as they are filtered through loneliness; and most of the impact of age is also filtered through loneliness.

It is also interesting to note that there is relatively little short-circuiting going on in the model. Most variables exercise their influence "further down the line," indirectly rather than directly. There are only three short-circuit linkages, the —.20 already mentioned between age and a desire to marry, the —.21 between age and loneliness, and the —.50 between age and modern values. Age, then, is the only variable in the model that is likely to cause short circuits. Of the twelve paths on the model, only three are short-circuit paths; the other nine are paths to the next variable on one or the other causal system.

If one asks why are priests inclined to leave the priesthood, our model presents the response that they are inclined to leave because they want to marry. If the question is asked why are they inclined to marry, the answer is that they are inclined to marry principally because they are lonely. The next question is why are they lonely? And the answer is they are lonely (to the extent that we are able to explain it) because they are younger, because they have more modern values, and because they do not like the work. If one pursues the lower causal system, and asks why do some priests dislike their work, the response is that work dissatisfaction is caused in part by the absence of religious experience, which is caused in its turn, in part, by coming from a tense family background, which is related to age. Turning to the upper part of the model, one may ask why some priests have more modern values, and we say that modern values are caused partially by age and by an inner-directed personality; inner-directed personality is caused partially by age, which relates to family tension.

There are a number of advantages to the model presented in Figure 3. First of all, it is relatively simple and elegant as social explanations go, and while social science is not at the state of the biological sciences and cannot say with Dr. Watson of the double helix, "If it looks pretty, it must be true," the elegance of our model gives us confidence that it is not a gross distortion of reality.

Second for all its simplicity and elegance, our model is complicated, both to describe and to understand. It is not more complicated than reality but much less complicated than reality. It is at best a schema of reality, and as a fairly complicated schema, of a much more complicated reality, it gives serious warning to those who wish to provide simple answers to complex questions. When someone says, "Why do men leave the priesthood?" and expects a one-sentence answer, the NORC team can only point to our causal model and say that the reality is even more complicated.

Furthermore, the model enables us not only to know what we know but to know what we don't know. The increasingly larger residual coefficients as we move from right to left indicate that while we are able to explain about half the variance in future plans and about one third of the variance in the desire to marry, we can only cope with about one quarter of the variance in loneliness. Given the fact that loneliness is the critical linkage in the two causal systems, it becomes obvious that in further research on the priesthood, the important challenge will be to explain why some priests are lonely and others are not.

Another way of examining the phenomenon reported in our model is to inspect the accompanying table (Table 3). In the first column of the table, the simple relationship between the various predictor models and plans to stay in the priesthood is presented. In subsequent columns, we see how this relationship is diminished when each new variable is inserted in the model, so that in the last column only one relationship, that between the desire to marry and future plans, is of sufficient size (above .15) to merit inclusion on the path diagram.

It should be noted that the model reduces the relationship between age and future plans from .44 to .04, indicating that we are able to explain most of this relationship. If we are asked why older priests are more likely than younger priests to plan to stay in the priesthood, we would say that the principal explanations for this phenomenon are that older priests are less inner-directed, have more "traditional" values, are less lonely, and are less likely to want to marry. Secondary explanations are that the older priests are somewhat more likely to have had religious experiences and to be satisfied with their jobs and somewhat less likely to come from tense families and to have high scores on the negative affect scale. If on the other hand the question is reversed and we are asked why younger priests are more likely to leave, we would reply that the principal explanations for this phenomenon are that younger priests are more inner-directed, have more "modern" values, are more lonely, and are more likely to want to marry. Secondary explanations for the relationship are that the younger are somewhat more likely to come from tense families and to have high negative affect scores and somewhat less likely to have had religious experiences and to be satisfied with their jobs.

We can also account for more than three fourths of the relationship between family tension and future plans. Those

TABLE 3 SIMPLE CORRELATIONS AND TOTAL INDEPENDENT
EFFECTS OF SELECTED VARIABLES ON FUTURE PLANS TO
STAY IN THE PRIESTHOOD

Variable	Simple Correlation (Pearson r)	Independent Effects of Added Variable (Standardized Net Regression Weights)								
		Age	Family Tension	Inner-Directed	Religious Experience	"Modern" Values	Work Satisfaction	Loneliness	Negative Affect	Desire to Marry
Age	.44	.44	.42	.37	.35	.22	.21	.15	.14	.04
Family tension	—.20	—	—.12	—.13	—.10	—.07	—.06	—.03	—.03	—.03
Inner-directed	—.28	—	—	—.15	—.16	—.09	—.11	—.12	—.13	—.08
Religious experience	.20	—	—	—	.15	.13	.09	.07	.07	.05
"Modern" values	—.47	—	—	—	—	—.26	—.26	—.20	—.19	—.14
Work satisfaction	.23	—	—	—	—	—	.21	.15	.14	.09
Loneliness	—.48	—	—	—	—	—	—	—.28	—.26	—.10
Negative affect	—.34	—	—	—	—	—	—	—	—.05	—.07
Desire to marry	—.66	—	—	—	—	—	—	—	—	—.47

who come from tense families are more likely to think of leaving
the priesthood because they have had fewer religious experiences, endorse more "modern" values, and are more likely to
be lonely.

The inner-directed are more likely to leave the priesthood
in part because they are more likely to have "modern" values
and in part because they want to marry. Those with modern
values are more likely to think of leaving in part because they
are more lonely and in part because they are more likely to
want to marry. Those with low-work satisfaction are more
inclined to leave because they are lonely and because they
want to marry. Finally, almost all of the impact of negative
affect is the result of loneliness.

We have chosen to use regression coefficients in our analysis
because they are the only feasible way to handle a multivaria-
ble model. One can use percentage tables up to three or four
variables, but beyond that number the use of percentage tables
becomes hopelessly confusing. Each simple correlation, for example, represents a whole table of percentages. However, it
seems appropriate at this point to introduce one percentage
table (Table 4) to illustrate the relationship between the desire
to marry and future plans with regard to the priesthood. (The
whole table is summed up in the r of $-.66$.)

One notes first of all that those who will definitely or probably leave are all concentrated in the two groups who would
certainly or probably marry sometime if they could. Furthermore, even the percentages for those uncertain about leaving are
much lower in the remaining three categories concerning possible marriage. Looking at the possibilities of marriage, among
those who would certainly marry, 70 per cent are either uncertain or planning to leave, and among those who would probably
marry, 36 per cent are uncertain or leaving. Among the remaining three categories, those who are uncertain or leaving
are 13 per cent, 2 per cent, and 1 per cent, respectively. There
cannot be the slightest doubt of the power of this relationship.

TABLE 4   FUTURE PLANS IN THE PRIESTHOOD BY DESIRE TO
MARRY
(Per Cent of Active Diocesan and Religious Priests)

Future Plans in Priesthood	"If celibacy for priests became optional, do you think you would ever get married?"				
	Certainly Yes	Probably Yes	Uncertain	Probably No	Certainly No
Definitely will not leave	11	16	31	55	93
Probably will not leave	19	48	55	43	6
Uncertain	35	29	13	2	1
Probably will leave	17	6	0	0	0
Definitely decided to leave	18	1	0	0	0
Total	100	100	99[a]	100	100
Weighted N	(3644)	(7830)	(10,176)	(17,548)	(24,033)

[a] Not 100 per cent because of rounding.

It would appear, then, from the analysis above and in the preceding chapter that the desire to marry is the main (though not the only) explanation of the inclination to leave the priesthood, and that loneliness is the main (though not the only) explanation for the desire to marry. We have much less success in predicting loneliness than we do future plans and the desire to marry, though loneliness is something much less specific than either of the other two. Apparently some men are better able to cope with the celibate life without encountering loneliness, and hence they are not so desirous of marriage and not as likely to contemplate leaving. Whatever the hidden causes of this ability to cope with celibacy without being lonely, they are not related to the personality variables measured by the POI scale.[We must be content, therefore, with saying that some men find themselves much more lonely in the priestly life than others; these are the ones most likely to want to marry and most likely to think seriously about leaving the priesthood.>

It should be noted that in order to determine whether other variables would provide more powerful explanatory force, three other variables were put into the position occupied in the model by work satisfaction—colleague relationship, professional comparison, and experience of power conflict. They did not improve the predictability of the model over the level provided by work satisfaction. Then all three of these variables were put into the model together with work satisfaction, but there was still no improvement in predictive power. In other words, we are not missing any relationships by using work satisfaction in the model instead of these other indicators.

SPECULATIONS

1. Probably the most obvious thing about the causal model presented in the previous section is that while the two causal systems are linked at loneliness, the impact of loneliness and indeed of the whole prior chain of causality is in its turn filtered through the desire to marry. The question "If celibacy for priests became optional, do you think you would ever get married?" was asked in a part of the questionnaire quite separate from the future plans section, within a context of possible changes in the celibacy regulation. Thus, the .66 simple correlation between the desire to marry and plans to leave the priesthood (standardized to .47 in the model) cannot be attributed to the fact that our respondents immediately saw a linkage between the two questions. As a matter of fact, they did not even know that we were going to ask them what their future plans were when they responded to the question of whether they would marry if the celibacy regulation was

changed. There is no escaping the conclusion, then, that resignation from the priesthood is strongly related to desire to marry, and in its turn the desire to marry is strongly—though not quite so strong—related to loneliness. Interestingly enough, problems with authority do not seem to play much of a role in the decision to leave the priesthood. Indeed, the authority variable was not even important enough to be included in the model. (Though one measure of authority, frustration, was tested as a possible substitute for the work satisfaction variable; it was found to be of less explanatory power.) Similarly, the influence of authority as a problem net of loneliness as a problem was only .10 on the desire to marry, while the impact of loneliness as a problem net of authority as a problem was in excess of .3. Squaring both these coefficients to get their explanatory power, we may say that loneliness as a problem is ten times more powerful as an explanation of a desire to marry than authority as a problem. Both authority and sexuality are important aspects of the present crisis in the Catholic Church and the Catholic priesthood. Authority is mentioned more frequently as a problem, but sexuality is more likely to lead to resignation. In a hypothetical model in which all those priests who would like to marry have in fact done so and left the priesthood, the authority problem would remain undiminished. In an opposite hypothetical model in which structural reforms eliminate the authority problem, the resignation rate would diminish only very slightly. While there is, obviously, a linkage between the two issues, it must be emphasized that relatively speaking they are independent of one another, and that a set of solutions which would cope with the one problem would have no necessary impact on the other.

2. But if those priests who wanted to marry were free to do so, would they be less lonely and less likely to resign from the priesthood? In other words, would optional celibacy lower the resignation rate in the priesthood? The answer is, it seems to me, that the resignation rate would certainly decline some-

what, especially in the short run. However, I am inclined to suspect that it would tend to stabilize around whatever is the annual resignation rate of Protestant clergy. Since 32 per cent of the Protestant ministers (as opposed to 23 per cent Catholic priests and 43 per cent of the Jewish rabbis) have, according to the Gallup study, seriously considered leaving the religious life, and since frustration and discouragement are mentioned as frequently by Protestant ministers as by priests and more frequently by rabbis as the reason for considering resignation.[3] One would suspect, therefore, that those factors inclining a Protestant married clergyman to consider leaving the ministry would very likely have about the same impact on a Catholic clergyman. In other words, we will never again return to the pre-1960 situation where resignation from the priesthood was virtually unthinkable. (Of course, some men did leave, but usually in silent disgrace.)

The possibility of marrying and remaining a priest would keep in the priesthood those priests who still want to do the things that most priests do most of the time. It would not keep in the priesthood, or at least not in the mainstream of the priesthood, those priests who are fundamentally dissatisfied with the sort of work that is required of priests. Given the fact, as we shall note in the next chapter, that only about one tenth of those who have already resigned would be willing to return to full-time ministerial work if they could do so as married men, one may tentatively speculate that over a long haul the net reduction in resignations occasioned by the elimination of the celibacy requirement might be rather small. I am not implying that therefore there should be no change in the celibacy requirement; I am suggesting that the argument that a

[3] Twenty-five per cent of the ministers, 24 per cent of the priests, and 34 per cent of the rabbis mention frustration and discouragement. Interestingly enough, 17 per cent of the Catholic priests say that they have considered leaving to get married, while 19 per cent of the ministers say they have considered leaving because of financial problems, since they cannot raise their families on such small wages.

change would appreciably diminish the resignation rate ought
to be examined very carefully. My own inclination is to expect
that a far more powerful argument would be that a change
in the celibacy requirement might have a much more positive
impact on the recruitment rate than it would on the resignation
rate.

3. We must resign ourselves to the fact that the old notion
that it was extraordinary or unusual for a man to change his
mind about wanting to be a priest no longer has much validity.
It was an idea that came into being in a society where there
was little change and where most men did all of their lives
the job they began with. Options were not around to be exercised. Once a priest always a priest, once a farmer always a
farmer, once a knight always a knight, ad infinitum. I am not
arguing against the theology of a permanent priesthood; I am
simply saying that sociologically and psychologically the world
is very different from the time when it was taken for granted
that people did not withdraw from the active ministry. Our
Protestant brothers adjusted much more quickly to the changing
circumstances and have provided ways for men to practice the
ministry in fashions quite different from the ordinary parochial
service. They have also enabled men to withdraw from the
ministry with dignity and respect while continuing to be important and valued members of the church. It would certainly
be desirable to lower the resignation rate, especially by enabling
men to stay in the ministry who really do want to practice
as priests in the mainline parochial ministry or in some form
of specialized ministry. We must also face the fact that men
may change their minds, even that they may do so under the
inspiration of the Holy Spirit. To try to keep men in the
active ministry who do not want to be there, when, indeed the
Spirit is leading them elsewhere, is unjust and intolerable, and
it is at the least uncharitable and foolish to treat these men
as outcasts from the Church.

4. As we shall note in the next chapter, it is not easy psy-

chologically to resign from the Catholic priesthood. While presumably it will become somewhat easier in years to come, it certainly will not be any easier than it is to resign from the Protestant ministry, and one imagines that there is a good deal of soul searching that goes into that sort of decision. I often wonder how much of the anger directed at ecclesiastical authority by some resignees is a compensatory mechanism designed at least subconsciously to justify the taking of a step against which all their training has warned them. The man who is tired of doing what a priest does and is convinced that he cannot find any satisfaction or fulfillment in that work finds it more difficult to resign than one of his Protestant counterparts. There is still some social disgrace and stigma attached to the resignation and also, one suspects, considerable guilt feelings within his own personality. One way to compensate for his ambivalence and uncertainty is to attack ecclesiastical authority and to denounce the Church or even his colleagues who remain in the priesthood.

I do not suggest that this phenomenon is widespread, much less that it is reprehensible; I am suggesting that it is possible, indeed quite likely, that some men would use such compensatory mechanisms.

I know of one particular case (and I am not asserting that it is typical) in which a priest and a nun in a middle-class black parish attempted to push their generally very responsible and respectable parishioners into an extremely militant position while at the same time making drastic changes in the policies of the parish and its school with no consultation with members of the parish. The response of the parishioners was at first patient, then negative, and finally hostile. The priest and nun concluded that the parishioners did not like them, would not accept them because they were white and represented a white racist Church. The priest, therefore, on a Sunday morning denounced his bishop and his diocese for being white racist and resigned from the priesthood. Shortly thereafter, needless to say, he married the nun. In fact, his successor who was also white but much more moderate in his militancy and much more democratic in his relationship with the parishioners was immensely successful.

Such incidents are understandable and inevitable in the present confused situation. Only when the Church develops techniques for dealing intelligently and sympathetically with men who wish to withdraw partially or totally from the ministry can we expect the numbers of such men to decline.

RECOMMENDATIONS

1. I agree with the majority of priests in our sample (54 per cent) that those resigned priests who wish to return to the ministry should be permitted to do so, at least to some form of part-time ministry, which is all that most of them seem to want. I do not expect that this will become a widespread policy at once, but I would like to see progress made in that direction. I do not see why some priests who have resigned to marry could not under certain sets of circumstances be permitted to exercise some forms of the ministry. However, I would agree only somewhat that the resignees should be permitted to return to the active ministry. I would think that the fact of resignation is an exercise of an option by an individual that gives the Church a right to exercise its option that while men should be considered a possibility for return, no one ought to be conceded an automatic right to return. The circumstances of his resignation, the maturity of his personality, the likelihood of his making a contribution to the work of the Church are all factors that should be considered, hopefully by some sympathetic but critical board of review. I think that return to the ministry is in its own way no more of a right than ordination to the ministry; in both cases the Church should satisfy itself of the appropriateness of its decision. Indeed, as I noted in the previous chapter, it is regrettable that there is not a system

of in-service evaluation by which the Church can determine whether a given clergyman ought to be permitted to continue the exercise of the ministry.

2. To be consistent, I must argue that those who resigned from the priesthood and do not wish to return should be permitted the opportunity to play the role of responsible layman in the Church—so long as they are willing to play the role. The former priest obviously cannot claim the right to be a supervisor of religious instruction, a superintendent of schools, or a catechetics instructor in a Catholic secondary school; at least he can claim no right to the job if he does not already have it; and I am inclined to think that he cannot claim a right to continue in the job he held before resignation.[4] Nevertheless, it seems inappropriate to me to refuse to hire a man for a responsible position as a layman merely on the grounds that he is a resigned priest. He has no more right to the job I would think that any layman would have, but he has no less a right. Therefore, the present prohibition excluding resigned priests from such occupations, however understandable it may be and perhaps even necessary in the short run, ought to be reconsidered in the immediate future. The only argument against eliminating this rule of any value that I know is that lay people might be shocked to discover a resigned priest occupying a responsible position in the Church. And again, they might not. The simple truth is that until we do more research on the subject of lay attitudes toward the clergy, we will not know.

On the other hand, I think the Church might reasonably expect that those resigned priests who are permitted to return to some form of the ministry or who are hired for responsible lay positions in the Church would be held to the same kind of organizational loyalty that is expected of mainline clerics. The day when loyalty meant that one dared not breathe a

---

[4] The case of college faculty members is another issue, and one which I am not prepared to discuss in this volume.

word of criticism even to oneself is gone, but any professional is expected to have a certain amount of loyalty toward the organization for which he works or withdraw from that organization. A priest, no matter what his clerical status, who spends most of his time denouncing ecclesiastical authority or challenging fundamental Church doctrines (and by fundamental doctrine I mean the core of the Good News of the Christian message), simply ought not to be a priest. Nor ought the Catholic layman who behaves in this fashion hold any position in the ecclesiastical structure. Other human groups are able to draw a line between responsible and irresponsible criticism; it is somewhat harder for the Catholic Church to do so, because until recently almost all criticism was defined a priori as irresponsible. Given the much more flexible structure beginning to emerge in the Church, we will have to become practiced in developing policies that lie somewhere between the one extreme where every critic is deemed worthy of purge and a policy in which every criticism, no matter how outrageous or destructive, will be tolerated and even encouraged.

Is the increase in resignations in the Catholic Church a good thing? The most immediate answer, I suppose, would be to say that it is not; the Church can ill afford to lose priests. But to an extent the upsurge in resignations is good; it does create a situation of greater freedom and flexibility for priests and does provide options for mature decision that were not previously available. It represents, at least from one point of view, a form of progress. The critical challenge, it seems to me, is to widen the options, for now a man can leave the priesthood and with some difficulty maintain both his self-respect and his relationship to the Church, but he only has two choices: to remain as a priest engaged in what I have called mainline priestly work or to leave the priesthood. One would like to see a situation in which a number of intermediary options were developed, including remaining in the priesthood but in specialized forms of ministry, or leaving the priesthood but remaining deeply involved in the work of the Church. Surely, the development of such intermediary options ought not to present any great difficulty or challenge to a Church that is becoming more flexible in its organizational structure.

12

RESIGNED PRIESTS

For reasons of causal analysis, the previous chapter was based on men who were in the priesthood and had inclinations to resign. The basic reason for this is that logically one cannot tell whether the attitudes and behavior of those who have already resigned from the ministry are either a cause or effect of the experience of resignation. In this chapter we will summarize our findings about those who have already resigned.

1. As the accompanying table shows, between 1966 and 1969, 4.9 per cent of the diocesan priests and 6.5 of the religious order priests had left the priesthood. If all of those who said they were certainly or probably going to leave had in fact done so by the end of 1970 (and we have no way of knowing whether they did or not), approximately 8 per cent of the diocesan and 9 per cent of the religious priests would have resigned since the beginning of 1966. Quite apart from what our respondents did, resignation rates between 1966 and 1969 would indicate that somewhere in excess of 3400 priests resigned during those four years.

2. While some resignees are angry at the Church, many others are not. Their emotions about the Church, their resignation, and their present relationship to the Church are mixed.

3. Approximately two fifths of the resigned priests still go to church every week and consider themselves to be active members of the Church. Another two fifths consider themselves to be Catholics but not part of the official Church. Only one

TABLE I   MARITAL ADJUSTMENT BALANCE SCALE SCORES
OF RESIGNED PRIESTS AND COLLEGE-EDUCATED MALES

	Mean Scores
Resigned priests (by year of resignation):	
1970	6.9
1969	6.6
1968	6.2
1967	5.8
1966	4.9
1964–65	5.0
Total	6.1
College-educated males (by age):[a]	
26–35	5.5
36–45	5.4
46–55	6.4

[a] Data from NORC Hapiness Study, 1963.

fifth feel that they are no longer a part of the Church. These proportions do not change very much as the number of years since resignation increases. If one accepts that a faith problem certainly exists for that one fifth who now no longer define themselves as Catholics, it is interesting to note that rejection of the faith does not grow more common as the years pass, at least so far as regular church attendance is any indication of continuing faith.

4. The most frequently mentioned reason for leaving the priesthood is a desire to marry; however, the number of priests who describe different sorts of problems with Church structures as the principal reason for resignation is far more numerous than those who mention marriage.

5. About two fifths of the priests are interested in a return to an active ministry, but only about one tenth want to return

to full-time priestly work. A minority preside occasionally over liturgical functions, but this liturgical exercise decreases as the resignation event recedes into the past.

6. More than eight out of ten say that they are very satisfied with their decision to resign, and this proportion does not change with time.

7. About one third of them make more than $12,000 a year salary.

8. Generally speaking, resigned priests report that they were treated rather kindly by their colleagues, their friends, their families, and their superiors during the resignation experience. The principal criticism was reserved for the delays and the obscurity of the laicization process.

9. Four out of five of the priests are married, eight out of ten of their wives are Catholics. Forty-three per cent of the wives were members of religious communities, 22 per cent more were widowed or divorced. Approximately half of the wives of resigned priests attend church each week.

10. Norman Bradburn and his colleagues have developed a marital adjustment balance score, which is somewhat like their affect balance score, by the combination of two positive scales of marital sociability and marital companionship with a negative scale of marital tension. The accompanying table shows the mean marital adjustment balance score for resigned priests by the year of resignation and compares it with college-educated males. In the years immediately after resignation, the marriage adjustment score for resigned priests is *higher* than that of the typical American male; however, with each added year since resignation, the marital adjustment balance score goes down. Those who resigned from the priesthood in 1964, 1965, and 1966 have scores that are lower than those of college-educated American males. The implication seems to be that the marriages of former priests begin at a very high level of adjustment, but that the adjustment deteriorates with the passage of time. However, only three of the priests reported that they were separated

or divorced—though there is some reason to think that others who may be separated or divorced might be reluctant to respond to a questionnaire. It may be that those priests who resigned five and six years ago are now at the most difficult period of adjustment in any marriage, and that their adjustment score will move up again, although their score is still lower than the youngest group of college-educated males who are also presumably going through the most severe adjustment crisis. If one looks at the component elements of the marriage adjustment scale for resigned priests, we see both that the indicators of tension are increasing and the indicators of sociability and companionship are decreasing. However, the sociability and companionship still remain roughly comparable with that of college-educated males; it is the tension scores that seem to be much higher.

Whether marital adjustment declines and marital tension increases because these men are former priests or whether it is merely because they are men who entered into marriage at a much later age of life than most Americans do is a question we cannot answer with the data available to us, since we do not have enough American males in our sample who entered marriage after age thirty. It would be an exaggeration to say that the marriages of resigned priests "aren't working out." One can say on the basis of our data that the marriages of those who resigned in 1964, '65, and '66 are showing clear signs of strain. What comes of this strain remains to be seen.

PERSONAL OBSERVATION

Speculations and recommendations about resigned priests are all contained in the previous chapter. I trust that I made it clear there that I think former priests should be treated with dignity and respect, and that options ought to be open to them to serve the Church either as priests or as laymen. I respect the decision to resign from the priesthood that any man makes, and I think that we must assume in each case that it is a mature decision, arrived at after considerable agony and representing an attempt at both personal and religious growth. Having said this, however, let me make it clear that I deeply resent the implication by some liberal Catholic lay people that the best priests are leaving or that the normal and healthy males are leaving the priesthood, or that only creeps and sexual misfits remain behind. I resent even more the attacks on the Church and on the priesthood by some—obviously a minority— resigned priests, and I am particularly angered that those resigned priests who argue (as James Kavenaugh has) that it is only sexual immaturity that keeps us in the priesthood. If I am expected to respect the decision of a man to leave, then I expect him and all his friends to respect the decision of the overwhelming majority of us who elect to stay. I firmly applaud the sympathy and compassion displayed by some laity to resigned priests; I would be more impressed with this sympathy and compassion if I thought they were at all interested in providing emotional support for those who elect to remain priests. (Just as my former pastor said there were "priest fans," so, too, are there "ex-priest fans," and some of them couldn't care less about what happens to those of us who remain. But should we show the slightest doubt or the bare beginnings of attempts to leave, they will swarm over us with kindness and concern.) To resign from the priesthood may be for some men a good thing, but to stay in the priesthood for most of the rest of us is a good thing. The implication of a good deal of the publicity about resigned priests is that staying in the priesthood is not a good thing.

I will confess (as one of my most sensitive priestly friends put it) to a sense of abandonment when a priest I know resigns. He is within his rights to do so, of course, and I will concede that what he is doing is mature and responsible, yet I miss him in the priesthood, and in the objective order his departure is a loss for the priesthood; in my own subjective emotions it is a loss for me as a priest. I assume, as I must, that he has taken all these variables into account in preparing the calculus that led to his resignation. He knows that the Church needs dedicated priests; he knows that the lay people need inspired clerical leadership; he knows that we who are priests need enthusiastic and vigorous colleagues. If despite all these things he still feels that he has no choice but to resign, well and good. As the Irish politicians would say, "Do what you have to do," but don't forget that there is tragedy in your decision—for the Church, for the laity, for your colleagues, and indeed tragedy for yourself.

I have no doubt that many priests go through exactly that kind of calculus; and with some of the resigned priests I know, I eagerly await the day when we will share the same active ministry again, though I would be less than honest if I did not concede that with some I would be less enthusiastic, and about a few I can easily say good riddance. (And my sympathies go to the poor women who make the mistake of marrying them.)

One must have compassion, respect, and sympathy for resigned priests, but it is not necessary to think that they are folk heroes, for they surely are not. They will not be the ones to reform the Church, they are not even likely to be the ones who force optional celibacy on the Church, for unless I misread the temper of the American hierarchy, that group of worthies are quite prepared to lose far more priests than it already has before it even begins to consider optional celibacy. If and when celibacy becomes optional it will be because of problems of recruiting rather than because of problems of resignation. The notion that the Church can be reformed from the outside is sociologically absurd, and the notion that one can force leadership to change by withdrawing from the system is politically absurd. The folk heroes of the present time ought not to be those who quit—however good their reasons for quitting—but those who stay to fight.

In the words of John L. McKenzie, "Why quit? Stay and bother them."

And in the words of Hans Küng, "Why should I quit? Let the pope quit."

There is a good deal of existentialist and psychological vocabulary used to discuss the problems of the priesthood, particularly the issue of resignation from the priesthood. Words like "growth," "self-fulfillment," and "self-realization" are used to explain and to perhaps justify resignation from the priesthood. In the face of the collapse of the old categories which prescribed appropriate attitudes and behaviors toward a permanent commitment to the priesthood, the new vocabulary of Freud and the existentialists has been very helpful in filling an intellectual and ideological vacuum. Unfortunately, the popular versions of existentialist psychology, rampant among clergy and religious in the United States, usually emphasize only one aspect of the psychoanalytic insights and the existentialist world view. Self-fulfillment is emphasized but self-transcendence is seldom discussed. The need for freedom is enthusiastically praised but little is said about fidelity. The human potential for growth is on everybody's minds and lips, but the tragic dimension of human life is rarely discussed. The psychological climate, in other words, in which many of the decisions to leave the priesthood and the religious life are made is profoundly optimistic about man and about human life. It seems, usually, quite innocent of a sense of ambiguity and tragedy. One cannot, for example, imagine Sartre or Camus writing a novel about a man's leaving the priesthood. The existentialism propounded by many clergy and religious, in other words, is only the "soft" dimension of existentialism. There is also a "hard" side of existentialist world view, a side which requires fidelity to promises and skepticism about one's ability to escape from ambiguity and tragedy.

It may be legitimate for a man to leave the priesthood because he is tired of being a priest and because he thinks he can find happiness in marriage. However, it ought to be said at least once that an attempt to justify such a resignation in existentialist terms is of dubious merit, for authentic existentialism would hardly approve of the withdrawal of a permanent commitment simply because one has grown weary. So, too, would the authentic existentialist inculcate profound skepticism about the possibility that marriage would notably reduce the ambiguity or the loneliness in which one lives.

However, the American Church was simply not prepared to deal with process philosophy and psychology. Caught as it was before the council in an ossified Aristotelianism, it was swept off its feet by a simplified existentialism. Many clergy and religious made the leap from shallow clichémongering of Thomistic phraseology to equally shallow clichémongering of existentialist phraseology. Self-fulfillment came to mean doing what one wanted to do instead of integrating into one's life the tragedies and the ambiguities of the human condition by an exercise of fidelity to one's own personal commitments. Furthermore, the seminaries easily became scapegoats, which one could blame for one's own lack of "emotional maturity." Regression to adolescent behavior was thus legitimated both on the grounds of the need to arrive at maturity and on the grounds of fighting against the tryanny of oppressive Church structures.

Not much attempt was made to point out that problems of emotional maturity are much more likely to be rooted in the preseminary childhood than in the seminary experience. (The point is supported by the data collected in the NORC study.) Nor was much made of the possibility that priests and religious might be no less emotionally mature or self-fulfilled than their lay counterparts. (Another possibility strongly supported by our data.) Finally, it has practically never been said that a retreat into adolescent behavior patterns is something to which many if not most Americans are tempted in the middle years of life. Because of their family responsibilities and occupational commitments, most American laymen are given but limited opportunity to indulge in such returns to adolescence, but priests and religious, freed from the commitments and structures of the past and not yet encumbered with family responsibilities, have much greater opportunity to relive adolescence and also an ideological justification for regression.

Let me emphasize once again that this is not intended to be a criticism of individual decisions to leave the priesthood or indeed a defense of other individual decisions to stay. My point is, rather, that a lack of solid theory of priestly commitment left many troubled clergy with no other set categories with which to deal with the problems of the present moment besides very inadequately understood categories of psychological personalism. Authentic personalism provides little justification for childish behavior, but shallow personalism provides marvelous legitimation for childishness and irresponsibility. All of us tend to be childish and irresponsible on some occasions, and in times of rapid change and crisis the tendency is even stronger. However, when we find ourselves in a traumatic transitional situation, without any clear norms to prescribe appropriate behavior, the temptation to irresponsibility and immaturity grows all the more powerful—especially when the shallow ideology which fills our theoretical vacuum suggests that immaturity and irresponsibility are positive virtues.

In fact, such personalist categories as fidelity and commitment can provide the basis for developing a powerful new theory of priestly dedication, and the sooner such theory is developed, the better.

I repeat that none of the last several paragraphs are intended to suggest that those who leave the priesthood are necessarily immature or irresponsible. Some decisions to leave are undoubtedly so, and some decisions to stay are also immature and irresponsible. Conversely, some decisions to leave are quite adult as are some decisions to stay. But the last point deserves to be repeated time and time again in our present confused transitional era: Resigning from the priesthood is not the only way to achieve self-fulfillment, much less self-transcendence. Those who remain in the priesthood, faithful to their initial commitments to the ministry, have every bit as much chance for rich, happy, and productive lives as those who resign. Fidelity, commitment, maturity, responsibility, in the final analysis, are not the result of whether one is a priest or not. They are as necessary in the priesthood as out of it, as difficult to achieve in the priesthood as out of it, and as possible in the priesthood as out of it. Such statements may be truisms and to make them would not be necessary if there was not a kind of conventional wisdom which in the name of a very shallow personalism dismisses the possibility of self-fulfillment in the priestly life. Whatever else the findings of the NORC study establish, they at least should put to rest such nonsense.

13

VOCATIONAL RECRUITMENT

FINDINGS

1. A far more serious problem for the Church than the resignation of priests is the apparent collapse of vocational recruitment. There are only half as many seminarians as there were just five years ago. Some of this decline may be the result of different patterns of seminary entrance, especially since there is every appearance of an increase in the last year or two in the number of men entering a postcollege seminary. In part, the decline of vocations may be a decline in the enrollments at preparatory and college seminaries.

However, it is not likely that any more than a small part of the vocation crisis can be explained away by new patterns of seminary entrance. Given the fact that priests themselves say that the most influential person in their own decision to enter the seminary was another priest, it is obvious that the vocational recruiting attitudes of priests are extremely important.

2. Priests were asked what their attitudes were four or five years ago and what their attitudes are presently. The decline is extremely sharp. Among diocesan priests, five years ago 64 per cent actively encouraged boys to enter the seminary; at present the number has dropped almost in half to 33 per cent. Among religious priests, the percentage four or five years ago was 56 per cent, today it is 27 per cent. It is not that

priests attempt to discourage young men from entering the seminary, it is that they are much less likely to enthusiastically recruit young men to the priesthood. On the four-point scale we created to measure attitudes toward vocational recruiting, there has been in the last four or five years a change among 42 per cent of the priests, with 4 per cent saying they now are more encouraging than they were four or five years ago and 38 per cent saying they are less encouraging. This could be the most chilling finding in our entire report. Recruitment to the priesthood depends principally on encouragement from men who are already priests, and if the priests in the United States are notably less encouraging now than they were four or five years ago, the Catholic priesthood is in serious trouble. The findings of high morale among priests reported in a previous chapter seem less important if these men are not recruiting replacements.

Furthermore, this decline in vocational enthusiasm seems to pervade the priesthood and is not limited to any one particular group. Our causal model, which was so successful in explaining resignations, can only explain 16 per cent of the variance on the vocational recruiting scale. When ten variables (the eight on the model plus negative affect and the inclination to stay in the priesthood) can only explain 16 per cent of the variance, the model really isn't worth very much. It is worth noting, too, that there is not much of a negative relationship between being a young priest and encouraging vocations. The relationship between age and vocation encouragement is only .14. In other words, older clergy are not much more likely than younger ones to encourage young men to enter the priesthood. It may very well be true that in the pre-Vatican Church, it was precisely the younger clergy who were the most likely to do the vocational recruiting. The seminary crisis at the present time may be the result of the younger clergy being no more likely to recruit than older clergy. In other words, the decline in recruiters has taken place precisely among that group where in the past recruitment efforts were most likely to be concentrated.

SPECULATIONS

1. My hunch is that it is precisely the uncertainty of the present times in the priesthood that have made priests hesitant about recruiting replacements. Since one does not know what things are going to be like in five or ten years, and since there are few scholars and leaders to provide a sense of direction, one may be hesitant about asking others to accept uncertainties and confusions. In a way, of course, this is a self-fulfilling prophecy; if men do not have confidence in the future of the priesthood, the fact that they do not recruit replacements ensures a very grim future. Priests may experience a very high level of psychological well-being and still be extremely dubious about what the future holds, if not for them personally at least for those who come after.

It is fashionable among certain conservative ecclesiastical leaders to blame the decline in vocation on the materialism or the softness of American youth or the collapse of the values of the American Catholic family. One ought to be wary of such an explanation (as one should be of any self-serving explanation), but this particular form of self-serving, sloganeering seems even less appropriate when one considers that but a decade ago vocational recruitment was at an all-time high. The American Catholic family has collapsed in the last decade? Young people have become dramatically more materialist and sensualist in the last decade? Nonsense.

A much more plausible explanation is that changing attitudes and values in the lay population, especially in the young lay population, are of considerable less importance in explaining the decline of vocation than is the curtailment of recruiting activity by priests. Of course if priests are not confident about the future of the priesthood, this lack of confidence will infect the laity, especially the young laity. It is very unlikely that there has been no change in attitudes toward vocations among the Catholic laity; an absence of change would be astonishing given the wide publicity about the present crisis in the priesthood. But until more research is done about the current attitudes of the laity, I will hold as a tentative conclusion the explanation that most of the decline in vocations can be attributed to a lack of recruiting effort by priests.

2. It may well be that in a Church provided over by episcopal leadership, the behavior of the bishop and the impact of his personality on his flock would be a strong predictor of vocational recruitment in his diocese. I am told that this has been the experience of the Anglicans and the Methodists. While there are some men in the American hierarchy who would inspire young people to follow after them, it must be confessed that there are not many of them, if any. The best that can be said of any hierarch is that one would want to keep him as far away from young people as possible. My own hunch is that if the Lords Spiritual wish to explain the decline of vocations, they stop blaming young people and Catholic parents long enough to take a good long, hard look at themselves in the mirror. In the absence of much more detailed research on the attitudes of the laity, especially the young, toward the organized Church, one cannot assert that large numbers of young laity view their bishops as phonies. But I would not be terribly surprised if such research (were it ever done) showed they did.

Until we have firm statistical data, it does not seem unreasonable to speculate that the image of the Roman Catholic priest is not particularly good with the young Catholic laity at the present time. Not so long ago, the priest was a figure of almost universal respect, both inside the Church and outside. Granted this respect was overblown and granted that it was in part an attempt to isolate the priest, to keep him at a distance, it nonetheless assured a young man that if he became a priest there was some dignity and integrity in his choice. But in the Church of recent years, all of this has changed. The young man may very well hear of complaints, expressions of frustration, and dissatisfaction from his parish curate. If he is in the seminary it is most unlikely that he can escape the influence of the restlessness and discontent that affect some seminary faculty members. And unless he is completely insulated from the mass media, it is hard for him to avoid seeing and hearing former priests or about-to-be former priests telling their sad tales of loneliness and unhappiness. If the priesthood is in such bad shape that large numbers of people are leaving it and many others are miserable, lonely, and unhappy as priests, why should a young man seriously consider the priesthood?

One might argue with a young man that our data show that the majority of priests are not unhappy and that on the average priests are happier than college-educated American males in the same age brackets. One might also argue that the media are not likely to seek out happy, satisfied, and fulfilled clergymen because these sorts of priests are not news. One might also mention that for a young man with vigor, confidence, integrity, and faith the priesthood can provide a more challenging and satisfying vocation than it has for centuries. Nevertheless, the fact remains that the young man hears the malcontents and hears those with the doubts and the hesitations. He hears the leaders of priests' organizations who attempt to use the threat of massive resignations, implicitly at least, as a bargaining club against the hierarchy. He is most unlikely to hear from those who are happy and satisfied in the priesthood, for, as the data of our study show, even those who are quite content in the priesthood now seem reluctant to vigorously recruit young men for the ministry. I suspect that those who are frustrated and unhappy not only dominate the media, they also dominate the atmosphere of the clerical environment to such an extent that those of us who are reasonably satisfied with our choices and have no intention of leaving the priesthood are reduced to silence most of the time. When an articulate and suffering minority is so acutely unhappy, it somehow or other seems inappropriate for us to assert that we are happy; it is even less appropriate to try to convince young men that they should think about the possibilities of the priesthood.

Furthermore, even though we may be convinced that the priesthood has a future for us personally, the uncertainty, the turbulence, the discontent raise some questions about the long-range future of the priesthood. It is all right for *us*, indeed quite satisfying for *us*, but who knows what things will be like in twenty years? Might it not be irresponsible for us to vigorously urge young men to join us in the priesthood?

High-pressure vocational recruiting is not likely to be very effective. Young people are both sophisticated and cynical about the "hard sell." In the long run, only the reorganization of Church structures and the effective reformulation of the Christian message will attract more young men to the ministry; of the two, reorganization of Church structures seems to me to be of lesser importance. I very much doubt that young men pondering the possibility of lifelong commitment to the priesthood are greatly impressed by the constant complaining and criticism of many of the priests' organizations. I further doubt that they are much attracted by the ongoing battle between the clergy and the hierarchy. It is not my intention to say that this conflict ought therefore to be terminated, but I think that those of us who engage in such controversy should be aware that when it is our principal concern and activity, it degrades the image of the profession. The priest who attracts young men to follow him into the ministry is not the one who throws a picket line around a chancery office; he is rather the one who can speak effectively of his vision of the goals and the values of human life and who presides in gracious love over the community of believers he has gathered around himself. In the final analysis, the only solution to the vocation problem is dedicated, joyous, enthusiastic priests who know what they believe and who are not afraid to speak their faith with clarity and conviction. They are also not afraid to live lives of hope, generosity, and trust.

RECOMMENDATIONS

1. It would be criminally negligent, given the importance of the priesthood for the work of the Church, for the leadership of the Church not to commission extensive research on the origin and the cures of the present vocational problem. If the leadership is not going to commission such research, and I personally am inclined to think they will not, then the priest associations should. For the priest associations not to be deeply concerned about attracting young men to the priesthood is as professionally irresponsible as it would be for the American Medical Association not to be concerned about recruiting young men to be doctors.

2. If the hierarchy and clergy are too interested in fighting one another, then I would hope that the various lay organizations of the country would become concerned with the problem. I presume that most Catholic laity want enough priests to go around in years to come. If so, they ought to face the fact that at the present rate there will not be, and that by the year 2000, if not before, the shortage of priests in the United States may be as acute as in the most de-Christianized sections of Europe.

3. Finally, priests should ask themselves whether in fact the decline in enthusiasm for recruiting young men into the priest-hood is justified. Granted that the confusion in the Church and the paucity of leadership and theory are acute, have we not become unduly pessimistic about the future of the Church and permitted our pessimism to become a self-fulfilling prophecy?

CONCLUSION

When the NORC team made its preliminary report to the sponsoring committee of bishops, one bishop asked, "After having worked on this study for two years and analyzed the data in great length, are you optimistic or pessimistic about the future of the priesthood?"

The question took me aback. However, since the bishop raised it the question has been on my mind constantly. I suppose the only answer is that I am both optimistic and pessimistic. There is perhaps no better way to conclude this book than to list the grounds for both optimism and pessimism.

First of all, I think there are a number of grounds for pessimism in the explicit data of our research:

1. A considerable number of American priests have resigned. Many more are likely to resign. There is no reason to think that the resignation rate is going to taper off in the immediate future.

2. Even more seriously, vocations to the priesthood have declined, in part, it would seem, because of the lack of enthusiasm about vocational recruiting among priests.

3. There are obvious strains and stresses between priests and their leaders on matters of authority and sexuality.

4. A minority, and by no means a minute minority, of priests are weary, discouraged, and disillusioned.

5. There are a considerable number of matters on which priests and bishops think very differently.

6. While there is not a generation gap in the narrow sense of the word, there are still many differences in vocabulary and attitude that separate younger clergy from older clergy.

7. A great many priests apparently do not find their talent challenged in the work they do.

In addition to these obvious grounds for pessimism in the study, in my own reflections and speculations on the data, I come up with a number of other causes of pessimism:

1. The old ecclesiastical structures, both of belief and organization, did not gradually evolve into new ones; they collapsed almost overnight and nothing has yet arisen to replace them.

2. There is a serious, perhaps fatal, absence of both leadership and scholarship in the priesthood and the Church.

3. Because of number one and number two, there is much confusion and uncertainty, hesitation, and doubt among priests, and the confusion at least is likely to be with us for the rest of the century.

4. Because of the confusion and uncertainty it is very likely that we will lose valuable traditions, customs, and institutions which in a different kind of transitional process would not be lost.

5. Confrontations between bishops and clergy are likely to grow more serious. The study itself, in fact, was a cause of friction, the National Federation of Priests' Councils finding it necessary to commission its own study because it did not trust the study that was done by the bishops.

The picture, of course, is not all dark. There are many signs of strength to be found in our data; indeed, more than some of us on the survey staff expected to find:

1. We did not discover emotional immaturity among priests when they were compared with other groups of typical American males. Neither their seminary years nor the absence of a marriage relationship has doomed priests to permanent emotional immaturity.

2. Priests evaluate themselves much more highly in terms of professional standards than I for one would have expected.

3. The emotional well-being—that is to say, the morale—of

priests is quite high, higher indeed than that of typical American males of the same age and the same educational background.

4. Many priests seem strongly committed to continuing their education and to serious reading of both books and journals.

5. Despite the confusion and troubles of the present situation, most priests seem reasonably satisfied with their working conditions and colleague relationships.

6. While some priests are going to leave, most priests are not going to leave, and there is no evidence to confirm the liberal cliché that the "best priests are leaving."

In addition, my own speculation has produced one more argument in favor of an optimistic viewpoint:

The really astonishing thing, given the rigid structures of the pre-Vatican Church, the dramatic collapse of those structures, and the present state of confusion, is that so few priests have left and so many priests seem both happy and dedicated in their work. This is not to justify either the rigidity of the old Church or the failures of the leadership and scholarship of the new Church, but it is to say that commitment, enthusiasm, generosity have managed to survive despite severe stresses and strains in what can only be called the many serious failures of Church leadership.

On balance, I am probably more pessimistic than optimistic in the short run. As I reread the recommendations that I made in the concluding section of each of the preceding chapters, I'm struck by the fact that most of them are not likely to become realities in my lifetime or, indeed, in the lifetime of most of us who are presently priests. I don't have much doubt that over the long haul, of course, the things I recommend will come to be, but in the long run, as Lord Keynes remarked, we'll all be dead.

And in the short run, a lot is going to be lost—the warm relationship between clergy and laity, the loyalty and dedication of the immigrant parish, the immensely important Catholic school system, celibacy, respect and admiration for the critical role that religious leadership plays in the life of people, understanding of the importance of the sacred for human condition, and the realization that order and stability are as important for human religious life as are change and growth; that indeed, without the former, the latter is not likely to be either healthy or successful.

I should like to be wrong in this conclusion. I have no doubt that all the values in these religious forms which I see vanishing will be incorporated in new religious forms at some time in the future, but they will be incorporated, I suspect, not through organic growth but only when another generation rediscovers them. The absence of leadership—both episcopal and clerical—the failure of constructive and creative scholarship, the lack of visionaries who inspire people instead of denouncing them—all these seem to me to be signs that the American Church and the American priesthood, as we have known them, are marked with the sickness of death. The Church is not going to vanish overnight, of course, and the overwhelming majority of American Catholics will continue to be Catholics in the same sense that the overwhelming majority of American Methodists will continue to be Methodists. But the vitality, the elan, the enthusiasm of the immigrant Catholicism is, I fear, headed for the grave. Many will rejoice in its death even though they have nothing better to offer. I disagree with their joy. It will take us a long time to replace what we have needlessly and foolishly lost.

We need men who can understand the traditions of the past and perceive the opportunities of the future. But there seem to be very few such men. Instead of leaders, scholars, and prophets, we seem plagued with careerists, faddists, and clichémongers. There are, of course, men of brilliance, charisma, genius, but not enough of them and not in the right places.

I would very much like to be wrong but if the Holy Spirit is going to prove me wrong, He has His work cut out for Him.